I0192786

PRAYERS
FOR MY CITY
A Fixed-Hour Prayer Guide for Wyoming

Steven Kopp

Series Editor
Jeremy Bouma

RENEW WEST MICHIGAN
Your purchase will help support
new West Michigan church plants.
Learn more at www.theoklesia.com/renew

PRAYERS FOR MY CITY: A Fixed-Hour Prayer Guide For Wyoming

"Preface," "Praying for Wyoming," and "Prayers for My City" prayers
copyright © 2012 by Steven Kopp. All other content copyright © 2012
by Jeremy Bouma

Published by **THEOKLESIA**
P.O. Box 1180
Grand Rapids, MI 49501
www.theoklesia.com

Visit online at www.prayersformycity.com

This title is also available as an ebook from
www.amazon.com and www.barnesandnoble.com

All rights reserved. No part of this publication may be reproduced,
stored in a retrieval system, or transmitted, in any form or by any means,
electronic, mechanical, photocopying, recording or otherwise, without
prior permission of the author.

Scripture quotations taken from The Holy Bible, New International
Version®. NIV®. Copyright © 1973, 1978, 1984, 2011 by Biblica, Inc.™
Used by permission. All rights reserved worldwide.

ISBN: 978-0-9854703-6-4

Printed in the United States of America

10 09 08 07 06 05 04 03 02 01

About **THEOKLESIA**

We are a hyperlocal idea curator dedicated to helping the Church of West Michigan rediscover the historic Christian faith for the 21st century. Jesus said that the Church is "the light of the world, a city on a hill that cannot be hidden." We provide the resources to help Her shine brightly in 21st century West Michigan by helping the Church connect God's Story of Rescue to our area, while remaining theologically rooted and biblically uncompromising.

www.theoklesia.com • info@theoklesia.com

THEOKLESIA
theology. for the church.

Contents

PREFACE   1

PRAYING FOR WYOMING   5

ABOUT FIXED-HOUR PRAYER   11

USING THIS PRAYER GUIDE   17

SUNDAY PRAYERS   21

MONDAY PRAYERS   37

TUESDAY PRAYERS   53

WEDNESDAY PRAYERS   69

THURSDAY PRAYERS   85

FRIDAY PRAYERS   101

SATURDAY PRAYERS   115

HOLY DAY PRAYERS   131

SCRIPTURE READING PLANS   159

Preface

As Pastor of Spiritual Formation, I have begun meeting regularly with the members of the church board. I've been asking the question, "What is one way you want to grow spiritually?" The most common response so far has been some variation of "I struggle with having regular times of prayer and Bible reading." I'm not surprised by this response for two reasons. First, it's a safe answer. Second, it's a legitimate concern to which I can totally relate. Personally, I have always struggled with keeping up regular patterns of meaningful prayer.

Now, this could lead me to one of two conclusions. Either our church is being governed by a particularly poor group of leaders, myself included, or these leaders are giving voice to an area of common spiritual struggle. I'm inclined to come to the latter conclusion, not only for self-preservation, but because I've encountered many Christians who, at various points in their lives, have struggled in this area as well. My hope is that this book can be a tool to help all who can relate to this struggle.

How Can a Prayer Book Help?

This is a prayer book. The majority of the content of this book is pre-written prayers; either prayers taken from Scripture (psalms, the Lord's prayer, the "Jesus Creed," etc.) or prayers shared by the historic Church. I was raised in a tradition that was suspicious of using prayers written by other people. Prayer, it was said, should be conversation. Since you wouldn't have a scripted conversation, why have a scripted prayer? There's certainly a lot of truth to this. Repetition in prayer can lead to a kind of formulaic spirituality where words are read and spoken, but are not accompanied by meaning. Or, perhaps worse, repetitious prayer can lead to a kind of supernatural belief in the power of the prayer itself. The statement, "if you pray the prayer of Jabez every day you will be blessed," gives power and honor to the *prayer*, not to the One who answers prayer.

But repetition does not need to lead to meaninglessness or superstition. For instance, I know many people that love the older hymns (some of which are contained within the pages of this book). They do not lose meaning over time or through repetition. Rather, they become sweeter. Or consider Bible reading. I have read many portions of Scripture countless times but I continue to read the Bible on a regular basis. The Bible is certainly not becoming meaningless to me with each repetition; it is becoming more precious. The same can hold true for prayer.

Since first picking up a copy of *Prayers for My City: A Fixed-Hour Prayer Guide for Grand Rapids*, the book that first introduced me to the idea of "fixed-hour prayer" (a topic of a later chapter), I began reciting daily from memory the Lord's Prayer. Now, this could certainly become a meaningless and fruitless activity in my life. But I have found that the exact opposite has happened. I have found that (surprise, surprise) God's Word has served to build into my prayer life more meaning and authenticity. As I pray through the Lord's Prayer, the Holy Spirit applies the truth of these words to my specific situation. I don't just say the words "Lord forgive us our sins." I confess specific sins in that moment. I don't just say the words "… as we forgive those who sin against us." I let go of anger or frustration in my heart. Just as the Holy Spirit applies the truths of familiar Scripture passages in fresh ways, the Holy Spirit also aids us in our prayers, even if we are praying other people's prayers.

As I mentioned before, my goal for this book is that it will become a tool to strengthen your prayer life. One way it can do that is by encouraging a balanced prayer life.

This book draws together a few concepts that, when applied together, build balance. For this I must credit Jeremy Bouma who developed the structure of the book and brought together the majority of the content from a variety of sources. Those elements are *Scripture*, *History*, and *Locality*.

This book is biblically rich. Prayer is not a process of emptying your mind. It is not a process of detaching from the conscious self. It is not a losing of the self in some kind of transcendent experience. Meditation in the Bible means contemplating, analyzing, and applying God's Word. It is centered on what God has revealed about Himself. The spiritual disciplines of prayer and Bible reading go hand in hand. Not only does this book include numerous Psalms and other biblical prayers, it also contains two reading plans for reading through the Bible.

This book is historical. It enters into the broad stream of the universal Church. Scot McKnight calls engaging in this kind of prayer praying *with* the church.[1] It reconnects us with the church of ages past and with believers all around the world who continue to engage in fixed-hour prayer. Again, I've spent much of my life skeptical of "traditionalism." In its worst forms it means legalism and dependence on man-made laws. But history also teaches. It adds continuity. It points us to the long work of God in the world. It reminds us that the Holy Spirit has been active in every generation, and will continue to be until Christ returns.

The two characteristics listed above are common to any prayer book that you might find. The "new" element in the books in this series is their focus on a particular location— in this case the city of Wyoming, Michigan. This is perhaps the most unique element of the book. For me, this grounds the prayers in a concrete reality. It reminds us that the

---

1 Scot McKnight, *Praying With The Church* (Paraclete Press, 2005).

transcendent God is also personal; that He truly does super-naturally intervene in space and time and that He does so in *our* space and in *our* time.

For Wyoming

Thus far, I've focused on the role of balanced prayer in spiritual formation. But the purpose of prayer is not solely for the one praying. No one prays for a friend who is sick for their own sake. No, you pray for someone who is sick because you want God to work in his life. You pray for your friend because you care for your friend and because you believe God can do something.

The "localness" of this book isn't a trick to ground our prayers in concrete reality. These are prayers *for* the city of Wyoming. Ultimately, we pray for our city because we care for it and because we believe God can do something on its behalf.

Steven Kopp • August, 2012

Praying for Wyoming

Introduction

Many of us understand what it means to pray for our daily bread, for forgiveness, or for someone who is sick, but what does it mean to pray for a city? How should we pray for the city of Wyoming? Before I sat down to write the prayers contained in this book, I knew I had to answer those questions first.

I took as my starting point the Story presented in the Bible. God created the world and declared it good. There was nothing broken that needed fixing. Adam and Eve lived in perfect fellowship with God, with each other, and with the world God had given them to rule over. The world was, in the truest sense of the word, blessed. But Adam and Eve rebelled against God and that rebellion resulted in judgment and brokenness. Every aspect of life was broken: our relationship with God, our relationship with one another, and our relationship with the earth. That early rebellion has continued and escalated through every generation since, vandalizing all of creation.

But the Bible is a story of both sin and redemption. God is also at work in the world restoring those broken relationships. The primary relationship that needs fixing is our relationship with God. And, by God's grace, we can be reconciled to God through Jesus' life, death, and resurrection if we come to God in repentance and faith in His Son. Redemption starts there but doesn't end there. He also reconciles us to one another and His presence and mission give meaning to all of our work.

As I constructed this prayer book for Wyoming, I wanted to consider each of these relationships and God's mission of redemption and re-creation in relation to the city, and to the specific needs of the city of Wyoming. There are a total of twenty-one prayers in this book. The seven morning prayers focus on our relationship with God. The seven afternoon prayers focus on our relationship with the world. The seven evening prayers focus on our relationship with one another.

Morning Prayers
When we look at God's relationship with "the city" in the Bible one story of "city transformation" stands out. It's in the book of Jonah. Jonah is a reluctant prophet who God finally brings to Nineveh. Jonah declares the simple message, "Forty more days and Nineveh will be overthrown." By God's grace, the people of Nineveh believe God and God shows his compassion on the city.

As Jesus approached Jerusalem shortly before His death, He wept over the city. He wept because Jerusalem had failed to recognize Him as Lord. It had rejected the true King. Jesus knew that the most important thing for the city was its relationship with God, and the key to its relationship with God was its recognition of and submission to Jesus.

Wyoming finds itself in the middle of Michigan's "Bible Belt." Churches are a common sight. The local church where I serve is across the street from another church. Go down half a block and you'll see yet another church. Keep going and you'll pass two more churches before you get to the first major road. Nevertheless, there is still a significant need for spiritual renewal. Some in Wyoming need to hear the gospel. Others need the Holy Spirit to wake them up from self-righteousness and complacency to the call of God in their lives. Many need God to lift them out of debilitating guilt and despair. God has work to do in the spiritual life of this city.

The morning prayers are pleas to God to restore His

relationship with the people of Wyoming. Since God has given the Church in general—and local churches specifically—the task of being the body of Christ to the world, many of these prayers focus on the life and mission of the Church: both through individuals living as salt and light, and local churches proclaiming the Gospel and demonstrating God's love. For Wyoming to be spiritually transformed God will need to empower the Church of Wyoming through His Holy Spirit, and Christians will need to respond with willingness and genuine love for their community.

Afternoon Prayers
God has revealed His goodness to the world by generously giving good gifts to all. Even though creation became subject to the curse and groans for its redemption, God continues to sustain and bless His creation. His general blessings are not limited to what we normally think of as the environment: air, water, trees, etc., (though Wyoming does enjoy its share of the beauty of West Michigan). God also blesses the world through human culture and institutions that make the city a source of joy and prosperity. The problem is that, just like our relationship with God is marred by rebellion and brokenness, so too is our relationship with God's creation.

The afternoon prayers focus on our relationship with God's creation, with work in general and with the institutions of the city, such as government, schools, and business. When functioning well, these institutions play important roles for the overall health of the city.

Wyoming, like the rest of the country, has faced some significant economic challenges. The strip on 28th Street has seen a number of businesses close or leave the city, even in my short time in the area. David, a church planter who grew up in West Michigan told me how 28th Street was the "place to be" when he was a kid. Recent years have not been so kind to the area. Unemployment, debt, and foreclosures are a big concern. This has put added strain on families already struggling under financial stress, and has a deep psychological impact on those unable to find work.

The schools of Wyoming are also busy adjusting to the changing dynamics of the city. A recent issue of the Wyoming Public Schools newsletter describes the consolidation of several schools. The newsletter reads "the Wyoming School District has seen significant change during its time, including changes in needs/use of aging facilities, demographics of our community, economic and job expectations, and graduation/workplace experience."[1] Many of the afternoon prayers are prayers for wisdom. In these challenging and changing times, community leaders of Wyoming need to find wisdom from God.

Evening Prayers
The evening prayers focus on our relationship with one another. One of God's acts of redemption is to heal those relationships. When we learn to love God we learn to love our neighbors too. And good neighbors (and families, and friends, and colleagues) are essential for a good city.

David, the church planter, confessed that when he was a child, he did not understand all the talk of "family" in the church. "Is it really that important?" he thought. Once he began his ministry in a part of Wyoming plagued by broken families and pervasive fatherlessness, a stark contrast from the environment in which he was raised, he came to realize the important role families really do play in the lives of children and society.

---

1 Tom Reeder, "WPS Prepare for Changes, Opportunities," *Insight: The District Newsletter for Wyoming Public Schools*, Spring 2012.

Other "relational" problems have crept into the city, such as crime and the emergence of gangs, often delineated along racial lines. Racism and classicism continue to be problems in the city, especially as Wyoming sees significant demographic shifts. A city worker told me the story of how a resident posted a comment in Spanish on the city website. At first he was encouraged by what appeared to be some new bridges between the city and its Spanish speaking residents. That optimism was short lived as another poster angrily attacked the Spanish speaking writer for not posting in English (even though the post was also translated into English).

The evening prayers also contain prayers for the handicapped, the elderly, students, and immigrants. While these are not specifically about "relationships" these groups often need especially strong relational support structures to be able to experience life at its fullest.

Prayer and Action
Prayer is one of the pre-requisite activities of Christian ministry. In the book of Acts the early believers regularly engaged in corporate prayer. But prayer is never the only activity of Christian ministry. It is always connected with word and deed. If you're reading this and have an opportunity to be an ambassador of God's grace in Wyoming (or wherever you are) take that opportunity. There are already many churches and community organizations doing good work in Wyoming and I encourage you to become involved.

We pray because we know that God is powerful to act. We act because we know that sometimes He acts through His people walking in obedience to His Word to proclaim truth and act with compassion. It is my prayer that the people of Wyoming will not only rise up in prayer for their neighbors, but that they will also love and serve their neighbors in

Jesus' name. Furthermore, ministry in the city will inevitably lead to more specific and relevant prayers that this book cannot provide.

Acknowledgment and Thanks

Wyoming is a complex city where the needs of one block are not necessarily the needs of another. Nevertheless, it is a city with a character and identity all its own. I hope that the prayers are relevant to this city and to its particular needs, though I acknowledge the limitations of such a short work. With only twenty-one prayers, the best they can be is representative. I want to thank several people for being willing to meet with me to discuss the book and offer suggestions for prayer. They are responsible for anything of worth and completely free of responsibility from any error I may have introduced. David Blok contributed insights from his experience as a church planter. Karen Vande Bunte, the prayer coordinator from OneWyoming graciously invited me to join her team in prayer. I also want to thank Tim Bos, our church's "missionary to Wyoming" for connecting me to others in the city and for inviting me to attend a meeting for the Wyoming Community Youth Coalition (WCYC). Finally, I would like to thank John Dubois, my pastor and mentor and my wife, Marj, for her moral support. Both offered early editorial advice.

I offer this book to the Church in the city of Wyoming. May God continue to use His Church in prayer and action for His glory and for the good of the city. I invite you to join me in praying for Wyoming.

About Fixed-Hour Prayer

You are holding in your hands a guide to one of the most historic practices in the Church. For thousands of years, God's people have come to Him throughout the day to offer praise, confess their sin, and cry out on behalf of others and themselves. They have joined with others around the world and across the ages to pray with one voice several times a day. This spiritual practice is known as fixed-hour prayer. It helps anchor us in Christ Himself as we participate in His Body, which in turn provides an oasis amidst the chaos of our week and reorients our lives around the Eternal.

That's what fixed-hour prayer does, because that's what the historic Church does: it reorients us because it anchors us. As our lives become more cluttered and multi-tasked thanks to modern culture, and as our spiritual lives become more slick and "progressive" thanks to the modern Church, we need an anchor. That anchor is the historic Church and one of its tethers is fixed-hour prayer.

Fixed-hour prayer acts as an anchor because it causes us to adjust our own personal prayer lives to the sacred rhythms of the Church and Her praying tradition. It's what one teacher calls "praying with the Church." As he says, "When Christians pray at fixed times with set prayers, they join millions of Christians scattered across the globe who routinely pause two or three times or more a day to pray what other Christians are praying. We are joining hands and hearts with millions of other Christians to say the same thing at the same time. By doing this we are creating in our lives a sacred rhythm of prayer."[1] We are praying *with* the Church, instead of simply praying *in* the Church as individuals.

For centuries, the Church has written down prayers and has

1 Scot McKnight, *Praying With The Church* (Paraclete Press, 2005), 1-2.

always prayed at fixed times with set prayers throughout the day. In the life of the early church, such gatherings consisted of almost the same elements as Jewish prayer times: reciting or chanting the Psalms; reading the Old Testament, to which was soon added the Gospels, Acts, and Epistles; and singing songs, composed or improvised. From the early church and through the Middle Ages, Reformation, and even the 20th century, fixed-hour prayer has been an important part of personal and communal spiritual practices.

Something has happened with this practice, though. We've lost something in our technological and cultural evolution; a grounding in the wider, deeper streams of the community of Jesus and historic Church practices has been forsaken. As we move into sleeker forms of Church and more technologically savvy worship environments, a tethering to our deep historic past continues to fray. As society has become multi-tasked and cluttered, commitment to spiritual disciplines has waned and prayer is considered a waste of time.

We need to recapture fixed-hour prayer for the 21st century in order to re-root and reunite the Church in the historic Christian faith, while also providing people an oasis amidst the chaos of modern life. This book is meant to help you discover—and, perhaps, rediscover— this ancient spiritual practice, while connecting it to your 21st century Wyoming life, too.

For many, fixed-hour prayer is an unknown practice. And for those who are familiar with it, you may have dismissed this discipline long ago as something entirely mechanical and impersonal. That's the case for many church traditions who think prayer would be reduced to something that was vainly and meaninglessly repetitious. This does not need to be the case, however. Some would argue that if any prayer becomes vain repetition—fixed or spontaneous—it's because our own heart isn't engaged, rather than what we say or how we say it.

What is fixed-hour prayer, then? How has it been practiced throughout the Church's history? There is a solid historical, biblical, theological, and practical foundation to this spiritual practice, one that has enriched the lives of countless followers of Jesus and rooted the Church of Jesus Christ for two millennia.

The Church has long considered ordered prayers during the day a practice that is rooted in the Holy Scriptures themselves. As the Psalm declares: "Seven times a day I praise you for your righteous laws" and "Evening, morning and noon I cry out in distress..." The life and story of Daniel illustrates how important this practice of fixed prayer was to the Israelites. In Daniel 9 we read that he followed the Jewish customs of praying three times a day, even though he knew it would kill him. Throughout the Old Testament, we see how important the practice of fixed-hour prayer was to God's people, the Israelites.

Israel was committed to praying when they got up, in the middle of the day, and when they went to bed, because this is what their Scriptures taught. In fact, Jesus Himself would have engaged in this practice. As a pious Jew it would have been impossible for Him to have not participated with all of Israel in this sacred rhythm. In the prayer life of Jesus we see three very important elements: the Psalms, the Jesus Creed, and the Lord's Prayer.

The Psalms were the backbone of this sacred Jewish tradition, and Jesus' entire life would have been bathed in them. They were carried over by the apostles themselves and were deeply foundational for their own times of prayer, remaining so still today. In addition to the Psalms, Jesus would have included what one author calls *The Jesus Creed*, which is an adaptation of the Jewish *Shema* and amended by Jesus for His followers. At least twice a day, faithful Jews would recite "Hear O Israel! The Lord our God, the Lord is one. Love the Lord your God with all your heart and with all your soul and with all your mind and with all your strength." Jesus, though, added a second part: "Love your neighbor as yourself." Lastly, Jesus would have prayed the very words He taught His disciples to pray, the so-called *Lord's Prayer*. Jesus told His followers to pray these words whenever they prayed, especially together in community; He would have, too. The Psalms, Jesus Creed, and Lord's Prayer. These three elements shaped Jesus' own prayer life, which was an adaptation of His own Jewish tradition. And these three elements have been shaping the Church's prayer life for centuries.

As is clear from history, fixed-hour prayer has been part of the Christian tradition from the very beginning. Along with the Lord's Supper, fixed-hour prayer is considered the oldest form of Christian spirituality. Early practicers of this spiritual discipline were trying to follow Paul's exhortation to "pray without ceasing," in addition to the psalmist's example to pray to God seven times a day. Many of the church fathers of the second and third centuries taught the practice of morning and evening prayers, as well as prayers at the third, sixth, and ninth hour. *The Didache*, a manual for Christian living from around the 2nd century, instructed the Church to pray three times a day. In his *Rule*, Saint Benedict of Nursia formalized fixed-hour prayer for his monks into what has become known as *The Divine* (or *Daily*) *Office*, which has continued in this basic form ever since.

Theologically, this prayer practice is unique because the structure is entirely God-centered. Whereas many prayers in gatherings and Bible studies are rightly petitionary or intercessory, fixed-hour prayer always is and has been exclusively an offering to God. Like the sacrifices of the Old Testament, this experience offers prayers of praise as a sacrifice of thanksgiving and faith to God—they are as sweet-smelling "incense of the soul" before God's throne.

Practicing fixed-hour prayer is a routine that takes an amount of discipline and commitment. Fixed-hour prayer takes seriously Paul's teachings in 1 Corinthians 9, where he calls on Christians everywhere to go into strict training and make our bodies our slave. (Re)discovering this ancient spiritual practice will help believers train themselves in order "to run in such a way as to get the prize."

This sacred rhythm is not a magic pill that will solve all of your daily headaches and life problems. It is, however, a time-honored way that Jesus Himself taught His followers to pray and how the historic Church has been praying ever since. And while many in the Church insist that we need to return back to the way the Church has always *believed*, I would like to suggest we also need to return back to the way the Church has always *practiced*, especially how the Church has always *prayed*. Perhaps re-rooting ourselves in the practices of the historic Christian faith will help re-root ourselves in the historic Christian faith itself.

Our world is speeding up, people are busy, and worship is considered a waste of time. Hopefully this book will provide an oasis in the middle of this chaos, and help you reorient your life around the Eternal.

Using This Prayer Guide

This prayer book is not just any prayer book. Think of it as the unofficial prayer book of Wyoming. It's a guide to help you, a proud Wyoming resident, pray for your city together with other voices. This guide is also designed to help you stay connected to your Creator and Redeemer throughout your hectic day. And this chapter will help you do both by walking you through the different pieces to this important historic Church practice.

The *Rule of St. Benedict* that formalized fixed-hour prayer for his monks in the 6th century prescribes eight separate prayer times throughout the day: dawn, 6 a.m., at the rising of the sun, 9 a.m., noon, 3 p.m., dusk, and at night before retiring to sleep. While keeping to such a regimen certainly disciplines the mind and trains the soul, for many such rigor is impractical.

Rather than offering eight strictly-timed sessions of prayer, *Prayers for My City* is a modified version of a well-known and widely used prayer book, *The Book of Common Prayer*. You may have heard about or used this book before. It is the official prayer book of the Church of England and used by many Christians in other traditions, as well. This prayer book has three daily prayer sessions: morning, afternoon, and evening. This format offers greater flexibility for the time of practice.

Instead of the normal 30-40 minute prayer services outlined by *The Book of Common Prayer*, this book has condensed and modified these sessions while retaining their central elements of fixed-hour prayer. Each day contains three 15-minute prayer sessions that combine liturgical confession, prayer, and Scripture reading, in addition to prayers specifically written for Wyoming. The prayer structure is meant to provide simple, yet meaningful, personal prayer experiences that help you stay connected to your Creator and Restorer throughout your busy day.

To get started, simply turn to the corresponding day and time of day (i.e. morning, afternoon, or evening). You may find first thing in the morning when you awake works well, or wait until your 10 a.m. coffee break. Lunchtime might be ideal in the day, or perhaps later in the afternoon would work best. Similarly, you might wait until bedtime to end your day in prayer or dedicate your after-dinner time to connecting with God. It really does not matter when you choose to enter into each prayer time. What matters is finding times that work with your life-rhythm and dedicating yourself to this spiritual practice of regular fixed-hour prayer.

You'll notice that every morning and evening session of prayer has required Scripture reading. This book provides two doable Bible reading plans starting on page 159. One plan is for the person who wants to read through the Bible in an entire calendar year. The other plan is for the person who may not have time to read the Bible in one year, yet desires to read through the Holy Scriptures from beginning to end. Either way, both plans will empower you to read through the whole Bible.

When you arrive at the morning or evening Scripture reading section, simply turn to the back and find the Old Testament or New Testament reading that corresponds to that day. Check boxes are provided for you to mark your progress or remind you where you left off. Consistently engaging in this daily rhythm of prayer will also help you consistently engage God's Word, even helping you read through it from beginning to end, perhaps for the first time.

Near the end of the book is a section called "Holy Day

Prayers." This section is filled with special prayers for specific days and seasons that correspond to the Church calendar, like Holy Week and Advent. Though not every day will have a Holy Day prayer, you are encouraged to add these prayers in the afternoon prayer session during its corresponding day or season. Many of these prayers are rich in history and meaning, helping you reorient yourself around the historic Christian faith and worship of God in the middle of your hectic day.

Finally, while this book is designed with independent, personal prayer in mind, you are encouraged to practice this ancient prayer-rhythm in community, as well. Though you may not be able to meet in a group for every prayer session, using this guide with your church small group, family, or even neighbors and coworkers will enrich your prayer times by praying for your city in one collective voice.

When using this prayer guide to help shape your prayer life please keep in mind two things: 1) you have the freedom to adapt this prayer practice to your daily rhythm of life, integrating it appropriately, while still preserving its frame-work; and 2) while this spiritual practice is meant to help aid you in your relationship with God by helping you main-tain a daily prayer rhythm, please do not be legalistic about this practice or get discouraged if you cannot keep the pace or fall behind. Think of fixed-hour prayer as your coach, not your task master. Doing so will give you breathing room and the permission to adapt the practice to fit your personal life, while also aiding your spiritual life along the way.

Hopefully (re)discovering fixed-hour prayer will help reorient your life around Jesus and His Way. Adapting this historic Church practice to your daily rhythm will lighten your burden, help you endure suffering, and keep your eyes fixed upon Jesus, so that you are able to run with persever-ance the race marked out for you in Christ.

SUNDAY
PRAYERS

YE THE LORD   WHILE HE MAY BE FOU

Sunday Morning

Philippians 1:2
Grace and peace to you from God our Father and the Lord
Jesus Christ.

The Jesus Creed
Love the Lord your God with all your heart and with all your
soul and with all your mind and with all your strength; and
love your neighbor as yourself.

Confession of Sin
Let us confess our sins against God and our neighbor.

Silence may be kept.

Most merciful God,
I confess that I have sinned against you
in thought, word, and deed,
by what I have done,
and by what I have left undone.
I have not loved you with my whole heart;
I have not loved my neighbor as myself.
I am truly sorry and I humbly repent.
For the sake of your Son Jesus Christ,
have mercy on me and forgive me;
that I may delight in your will,
and walk in your ways,
to the glory of your Name. Amen.

Lord, open our lips. And our mouth shall proclaim your
praise.

The Gloria
Glory to the Father, and to the Son, and to the Holy Spirit: as
it was in the beginning, is now, and will be for ever. Amen.

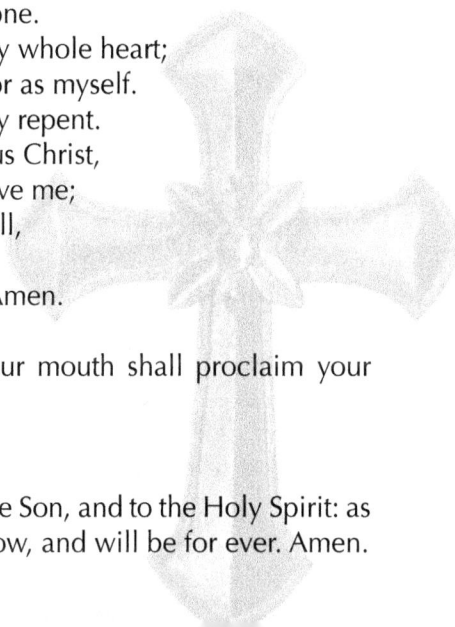

Worship the Lord in the beauty of holiness: Come let us adore him.

Venite—*Psalm 95:1-7*
Come, let us sing for joy to the LORD;
   let us shout aloud to the Rock of our salvation.
Let us come before him with thanksgiving
   and extol him with music and song.
 For the LORD is the great God,
   the great King above all gods.
In his hand are the depths of the earth,
   and the mountain peaks belong to him.
The sea is his, for he made it,
   and his hands formed the dry land.

 Come, let us bow down in worship,
   let us kneel before the LORD our Maker;
for he is our God
   and we are the people of his pasture,
   the flock under his care.

The Gloria
Glory to the Father, and to the Son, and to the Holy Spirit: as it was in the beginning, is now, and will be for ever. Amen.

The Morning Lesson
Old Testament Reading (found on pages 159 to 171)

The Morning Song—*A Song of Creation*
Invocation
Glorify the Lord, all you works of the Lord, *
      praise him and highly exalt him for ever.
In the firmament of his power, glorify the Lord, *
      praise him and highly exalt him for ever.

The People of God
Let the people of God glorify the Lord, *
　　praise him and highly exalt him for ever.
Glorify the Lord, O priests and servants of the Lord, *
　　praise him and highly exalt him for ever.
Glorify the Lord, O spirits and souls of the righteous, *
　　praise him and highly exalt him for ever.
You that are holy and humble of heart, glorify the Lord,
　　praise him and highly exalt him for ever.

Doxology
Let us glorify the Lord: Father, Son, and Holy Spirit; *
　　praise him and highly exalt him for ever.
In the firmament of his power, glorify the Lord, *
　　praise him and highly exalt him for ever.

The Apostles' Creed
I believe in God, the Father almighty,
Creator of heaven and earth.

I believe in Jesus Christ, his only Son, our Lord.
He was conceived by the power of the Holy Spirit
and born of the Virgin Mary.
He suffered under Pontius Pilate,
was crucified, died, and was buried.
He descended to the dead.
On the third day he rose again.
He ascended into heaven,
and is seated at the right hand of the Father.
He will come again to judge the living and the dead.

I believe in the Holy Spirit,
the holy catholic Church,
the communion of saints,
the forgiveness of sins,
the resurrection of the body,
and the life everlasting. Amen.

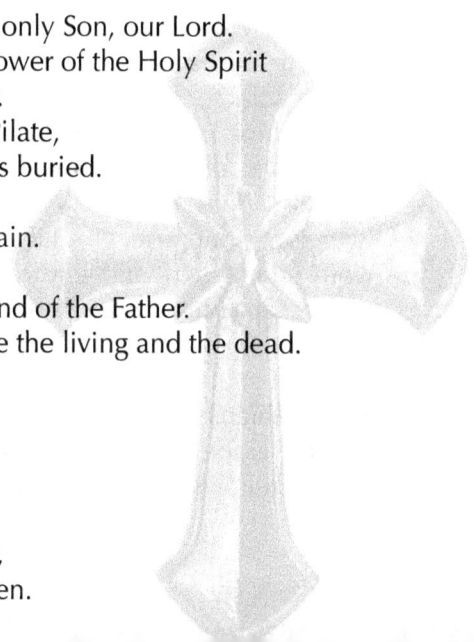

The Prayer of Our Lord
Our Father in heaven, hallowed be your Name,
your kingdom come, your will be done,
on earth as it is in heaven.
Give us today our daily bread.
Forgive us our sins as we forgive those who sin against us.
Lead us not into temptation, but deliver us from evil.
For the kingdom, the power, and the glory are yours,
now and for ever. Amen.

Prayer for the Day
O God, you make us glad with the weekly remembrance of
the glorious resurrection of your Son our Lord: Give us this
day such blessing through our worship of you, that the week
to come may be spent in your favor; through Jesus Christ our
Lord. Amen.

Prayer for My City (Romans 11:33-12:2)
God, you are worthy of all our worship. You are wise and
good beyond all measure. I pray for those in Wyoming who
gather together in the name of Christ to worship you this
morning. Please give us the grace to offer our lives as a
living sacrifice, holy and pleasing to you, in a spiritual act
of worship. Transform us by the renewing of our minds.
Help us to discern your will. I pray this morning that as
churches from all over Wyoming, and around the world,
offer songs of praise, give gifts for your work, listen to your
word proclaimed, and serve one another in love, that you
will accept our acts and our attitudes as offerings of true
worship. Amen.

2 Corinthians 13:14
May the grace of the Lord Jesus Christ, and the love of God,
and the fellowship of the Holy Spirit be with you all. Amen.

Sunday Afternoon

O God, make speed to save us; Lord, make haste to help us.

The Gloria
Glory to the Father, and to the Son, and to the Holy Spirit: as it was in the beginning, is now, and will be for ever. Amen.

Hymn Selection—*Before the Throne of God Above*
Before the throne of God above
I have a strong and perfect plea.
A great high Priest whose Name is Love
Who ever lives and pleads for me.

My name is graven on His hands,
My name is written on His heart.
I know that while in Heaven He stands
No tongue can bid me thence depart.

Hallelujah! Hallelujah! Praise the one risen Son of God!

When Satan tempts me to despair
And tells me of the guilt within,
Upward I look and see Him there
Who made an end of all my sin.

Because the sinless Savior died
My sinful soul is counted free.
For God the just is satisfied
To look on Him and pardon me.

Hallelujah! Hallelujah! Praise the one risen Son of God!

Behold Him there the risen Lamb,
My perfect spotless righteousness,
The great unchangeable I AM,

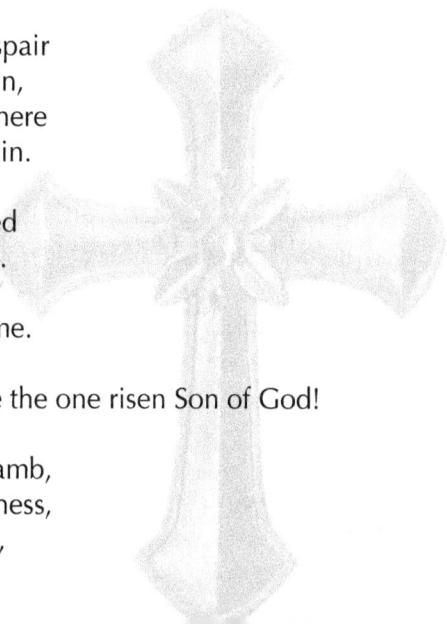

The King of glory and of grace,

One in Himself I cannot die.
My soul is purchased by His blood,
My life is hid with Christ on high,
With Christ my Savior and my God!

Psalm 119:105-112
Your word is a lamp for my feet,
   a light on my path.
I have taken an oath and confirmed it,
   that I will follow your righteous laws.
I have suffered much;
   preserve my life, LORD, according to your word.
Accept, LORD, the willing praise of my mouth,
   and teach me your laws.
Though I constantly take my life in my hands,
   I will not forget your law.
The wicked have set a snare for me,
   but I have not strayed from your precepts.
Your statutes are my heritage forever;
   they are the joy of my heart.
My heart is set on keeping your decrees
   to the very end.

The Gloria
Glory to the Father, and to the Son, and to the Holy Spirit: as
it was in the beginning, is now, and will be for ever. Amen.

Romans 5:5
The love of God has been poured into our hearts through
the Holy Spirit that has been given to us.

Silence
Lord, have mercy. Christ, have mercy. Lord, have mercy.

The Prayer of Our Lord
Our Father in heaven, hallowed be your Name,
your kingdom come, your will be done,
on earth as it is in heaven.
Give us today our daily bread.
Forgive us our sins as we forgive those who sin against us.
Lead us not into temptation, but deliver us from evil.
For the kingdom, the power, and the glory are yours,
now and for ever. Amen.

A few moments of intercessory prayer
Lord, hear our prayer; And let our cry come to you.

Holy Day Prayer *(found on pages 131 to 158)*

Prayer for My City
Father, you care for the poor, the needy, and for those who
hunger and thirst. I pray that you will provide for those in
Wyoming who are in need. I pray you will give them their
daily bread, clothes to wear, and a place to rest. I pray you
will grant them financial sufficiency. I pray that parents will
be able to provide for their children. I pray that you will
comfort those who are discouraged because they are unable
to find work and provide them with gainful employment. I
pray you will bless them so that they may bless others. I pray
that those who have financial means will be generous with
their fellow citizens and that they will give from a grateful
heart. God, please show me where I can be generous and
meet the needs of those in the city. Amen.

Prayer for the Afternoon
Heavenly Father, send your Holy Spirit into our hearts, to
direct and rule us according to your will, to comfort us in
all our afflictions, to defend us from all error, and to lead us
into all truth; through Jesus Christ our Lord. Amen.

Sunday Evening

Psalm 141:2
Let my prayer be set forth in your sight as incense, the lifting up of my hands as the evening sacrifice.

The Jesus Creed
Love the Lord your God with all your heart and with all your soul and with all your mind and with all your strength; and love your neighbor as yourself.

Confession of Sin
Let us confess our sins against God and our neighbor.

Silence may be kept.

Most merciful God,
I confess that I have sinned against you
in thought, word, and deed,
by what I have done,
and by what I have left undone.
I have not loved you with my whole heart;
I have not loved my neighbor as myself.
I am truly sorry and I humbly repent.
For the sake of your Son Jesus Christ,
have mercy on me and forgive me;
that I may delight in your will,
and walk in your ways,
to the glory of your Name.
Amen.

O God, make speed to save us; Lord, make haste to help us.

The Gloria
Glory to the Father, and to the Son, and to the Holy Spirit: as it was in the beginning, is now, and will be for ever. Amen.

O Gracious Light

O gracious Light,
pure brightness of the everliving Father in heaven,
O Jesus Christ, holy and blessed!

Now as we come to the setting of the sun,
and our eyes behold the vesper light,
we sing your praises, O God: Father, Son, and Holy Spirit.

You are worthy at all times to be praised by happy voices,
O Son of God, O Giver of life,
and to be glorified through all the worlds.

The Evening Psalter—*Psalm 63*

You, God, are my God,
  earnestly I seek you;
I thirst for you,
  my whole being longs for you,
in a dry and parched land
  where there is no water.

I have seen you in the sanctuary
  and beheld your power and your glory.
Because your love is better than life,
  my lips will glorify you.
I will praise you as long as I live,
  and in your name I will lift up my hands.
I will be fully satisfied as with the richest of foods;
  with singing lips my mouth will praise you.

On my bed I remember you;
  I think of you through the watches of the night.
Because you are my help,
  I sing in the shadow of your wings.
I cling to you;
  your right hand upholds me.

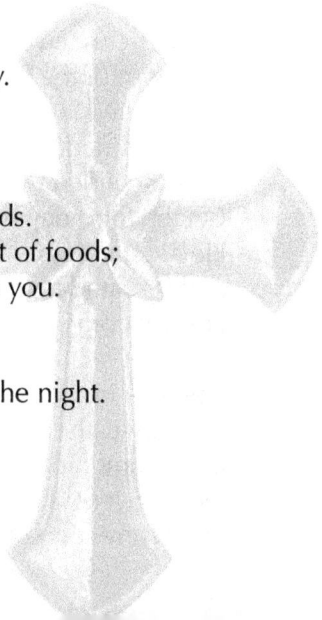

Those who want to kill me will be destroyed;
  they will go down to the depths of the earth.
They will be given over to the sword
  and become food for jackals.

But the king will rejoice in God;
  all who swear by God will glory in him,
  while the mouths of liars will be silenced.

The Gloria
Glory to the Father, and to the Son, and to the Holy Spirit: as
it was in the beginning, is now, and will be for ever. Amen.

The Evening Lesson
New Testament Reading (found on pages 159 to 171)

The Apostles' Creed
I believe in God, the Father almighty,
Creator of heaven and earth.

I believe in Jesus Christ, his only Son, our Lord.
He was conceived by the power of the Holy Spirit
and born of the Virgin Mary.
He suffered under Pontius Pilate,
was crucified, died, and was buried.
He descended to the dead.
On the third day he rose again.
He ascended into heaven,
and is seated at the right hand of the Father.
He will come again to judge the living and the dead.

I believe in the Holy Spirit,
the holy catholic Church,
the communion of saints,
the forgiveness of sins,
the resurrection of the body,

and the life everlasting. Amen.

The Prayer of Our Lord
Our Father in heaven, hallowed be your Name,
your kingdom come, your will be done,
on earth as it is in heaven.
Give us today our daily bread.
Forgive us our sins as we forgive those who sin against us.
Lead us not into temptation, but deliver us from evil.
For the kingdom, the power, and the glory are yours,
now and for ever. Amen.

Prayer of Suffrage
Show us your mercy, O Lord;
And grant us your salvation.
Clothe your ministers with righteousness;
Let your people sing with joy.
Give peace, O Lord, in all the world;
For only in you can we live in safety.
Lord, keep this nation under your care;
And guide us in the way of justice and truth.
Let your way be known upon earth;
Your saving health among all nations.
Let not the needy, O Lord, be forgotten;
Nor the hope of the poor be taken away.
Create in us clean hearts, O God;
And sustain us with your Holy Spirit.

Prayer for the Evening
Lord God, whose Son our Savior Jesus Christ triumphed
over the powers of death and prepared for us our place in
the new Jerusalem: Grant that we, who have this day given
thanks for his resurrection, may praise you in that City of
which he is the light, and where he lives and reigns for ever
and ever. Amen.

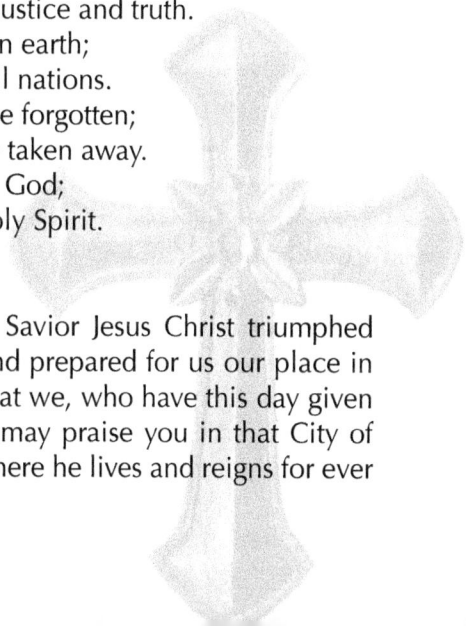

The General Thanksgiving
Almighty God, Father of all mercies,
we your unworthy servants give you humble thanks
for all your goodness and loving kindness
to us and to all whom you have made.

We bless you for our creation, preservation,
and all the blessings of this life;
but above all for your immeasurable love
in the redemption of the world by our Lord Jesus Christ;
for the means of grace, and for the hope of glory.

And, we pray, give us such an awareness of your mercies,
that with truly thankful hearts we may show forth your
praise, not only with our lips, but in our lives,
by giving up our selves to your service,
and by walking before you
in holiness and righteousness all our days;
through Jesus Christ our Lord,
to whom, with you and the Holy Spirit,
be honor and glory throughout all ages. Amen.

O God and Father of all, whom the whole heavens adore:
Let the whole earth also worship you, all nations obey you,
all tongues confess and bless you, and men and women
everywhere love you and serve you in peace; through Jesus
Christ our Lord. Amen.

Prayer for My City
Father, you have created the family as one of the most
basic building blocks of the city. I pray for families in
Wyoming. Make them strong and loving. Where there is
brokenness, bring healing. Where there is loneliness, bring
your presence. Where there is hatred and animosity, bring
reconciliation. Convict the hearts of parents to love, nurture,

protect, and care for their children. I pray specifically that absent fathers will turn to you, and return to their families. Turn the hearts of children toward their parents. Strengthen marriages. Finally, I pray that you will give single parents the strength and resources they need to raise their children well. Please fill the homes in Wyoming with joy and peace. Bring families together to worship you. Amen.

Romans 15:13
May the God of hope fill you with all joy and peace as you trust in him, so that you may overflow with hope by the power of the Holy Spirit. Amen.

MONDAY PRAYERS

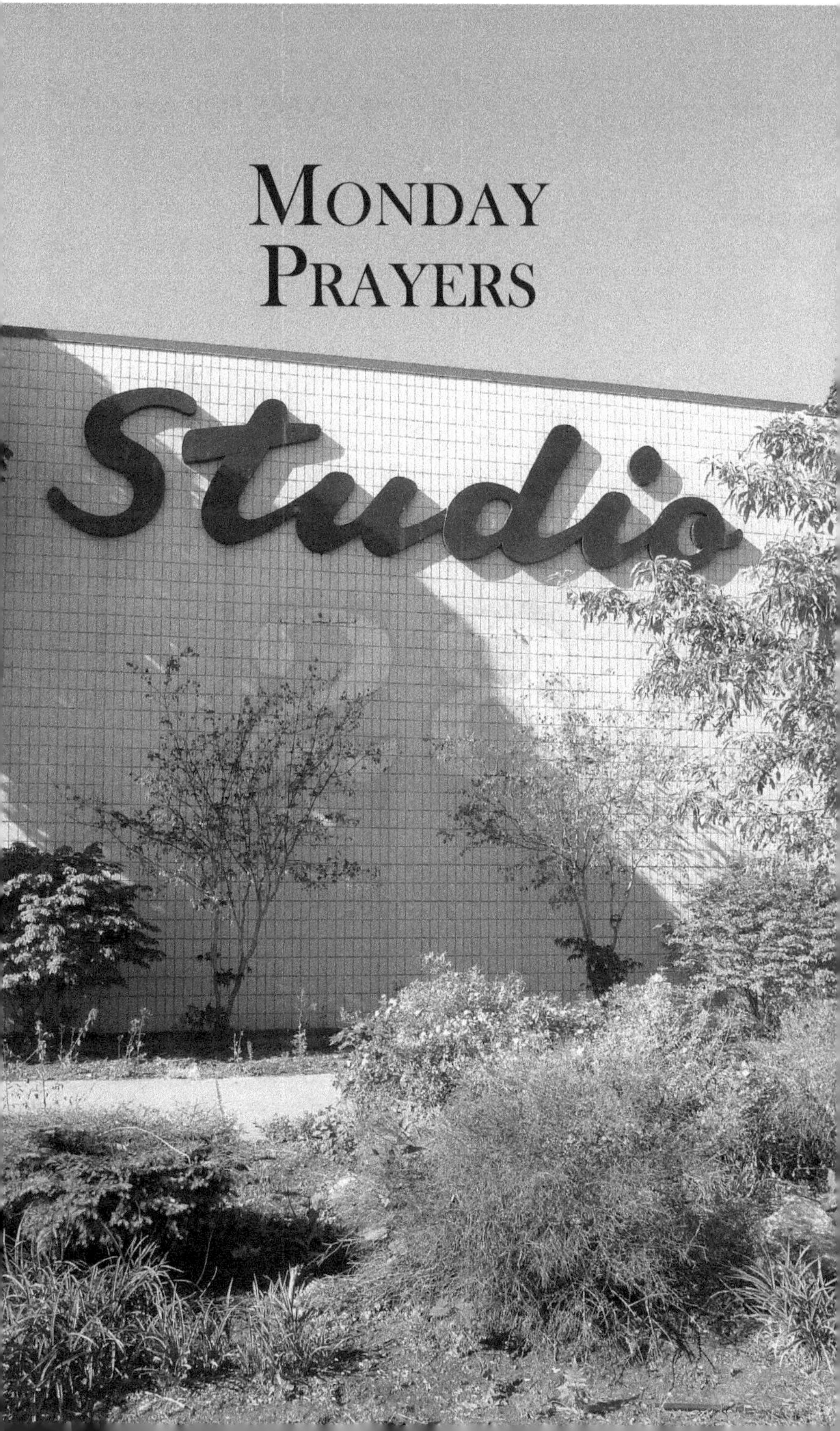

Monday Morning

Psalm 122:1
I rejoiced with those who said to me, "Let us go to the house of the LORD."

The Jesus Creed
Love the Lord your God with all your heart and with all your soul and with all your mind and with all your strength; and love your neighbor as yourself.

Confession of Sin
Let us confess our sins against God and our neighbor.

Silence may be kept.

Most merciful God,
I confess that I have sinned against you
in thought, word, and deed,
by what I have done,
and by what I have left undone.
I have not loved you with my whole heart;
I have not loved my neighbor as myself.
I am truly sorry and I humbly repent.
For the sake of your Son Jesus Christ,
have mercy on me and forgive me;
that I may delight in your will,
and walk in your ways,
to the glory of your Name. Amen.

Lord, open our lips. And our mouth shall proclaim your praise.

The Gloria
Glory to the Father, and to the Son, and to the Holy Spirit: as it was in the beginning, is now, and will be for ever. Amen.

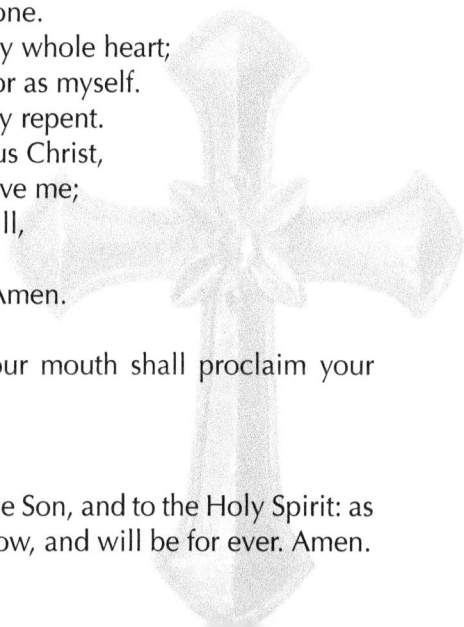

Worship the Lord in the beauty of holiness: Come let us adore him.

Christ our Passover *1 Cor 5:7-8 Rm 6:9-11 1 Cor 15:20-22*
Alleluia.
Get rid of the old yeast, so that you may be a new unleavened batch—as you really are. For Christ, our Passover lamb, has been sacrificed.

Therefore let us keep the Festival, not with the old bread leavened with malice and wickedness, but with the unleavened bread of sincerity and truth.

For we know that since Christ was raised from the dead, he cannot die again; death no longer has mastery over him.

The death he died, he died to sin once for all; but the life he lives, he lives to God.

In the same way, count yourselves dead to sin but alive to God in Christ Jesus.

But Christ has indeed been raised from the dead, the firstfruits of those who have fallen asleep.

For since death came through a man, the resurrection of the dead comes also through a man.

For as in Adam all die, so in Christ all will be made alive. Alleluia.

The Gloria
Glory to the Father, and to the Son, and to the Holy Spirit: as it was in the beginning, is now, and will be for ever. Amen.

The Morning Lesson
Old Testament Reading (found on pages 159 to 171)

The Morning Song—*The First Song of Isaiah (Isaiah 12:2-6)*
Surely God is my salvation;
   I will trust and not be afraid.
The LORD, the LORD himself, is my strength and my
defense;
   he has become my salvation."
With joy you will draw water
   from the wells of salvation.

 In that day you will say:
   "Give praise to the LORD, proclaim his name;
   make known among the nations what he has done,
   and proclaim that his name is exalted.
Sing to the LORD, for he has done glorious things;
   let this be known to all the world.
Shout aloud and sing for joy, people of Zion,
   for great is the Holy One of Israel among you."

The Apostles' Creed
I believe in God, the Father almighty,
Creator of heaven and earth.

I believe in Jesus Christ, his only Son, our Lord.
He was conceived by the power of the Holy Spirit
and born of the Virgin Mary.
He suffered under Pontius Pilate,
was crucified, died, and was buried.
He descended to the dead.
On the third day he rose again.
He ascended into heaven,
and is seated at the right hand of the Father.
He will come again to judge the living and the dead.

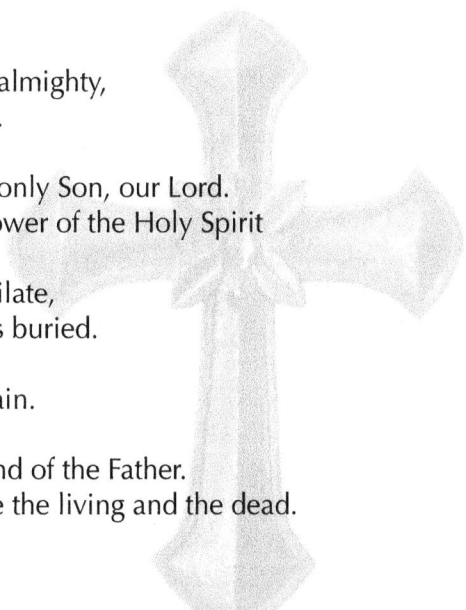

I believe in the Holy Spirit,
the holy catholic Church,
the communion of saints,
the forgiveness of sins,
the resurrection of the body,
and the life everlasting. Amen.

The Prayer of Our Lord
Our Father in heaven, hallowed be your Name,
your kingdom come, your will be done,
on earth as it is in heaven.
Give us today our daily bread.
Forgive us our sins as we forgive those who sin against us.
Lead us not into temptation, but deliver us from evil.
For the kingdom, the power, and the glory are yours,
now and for ever. Amen.

Prayer for the Day
Lord God, almighty and everlasting Father, you have brought us in safety to this new day: Preserve us with your mighty power, that we may not fall into sin, nor be overcome by adversity; and in all we do, direct us to the fulfilling of your purpose; through Jesus Christ our Lord. Amen.

Prayer for My City (Romans 6:15-23)
Father, you are the God who brings freedom. I pray for those in Wyoming who are held under the bondage of sin: for those who face addiction to drugs, alcohol, gambling, pornography or other addictive substances or behavior. Give them freedom from their sin and addictions. Protect their families and friends from the harmful effects that these sins carry along with them. Grant them the help and support they need. May they turn to you and become servants of righteousness. I also pray for those who are under the bondage of guilt because they have been trying to find salvation by following a strict set of rules. I pray that

they will hear the gospel of freedom in Christ, believe, and find new life in you. Amen.

Romans 15:13
May the God of hope fill you with all joy and peace as you trust in him, so that you may overflow with hope by the power of the Holy Spirit. Amen.

Monday Afternoon

O God, make speed to save us; Lord, make haste to help us.

The Gloria
Glory to the Father, and to the Son, and to the Holy Spirit: as it was in the beginning, is now, and will be for ever. Amen.

Hymn Selection—*Tis So Sweet To Trust In Jesus*
'Tis so sweet to trust in Jesus,
and to take him at his word;
just to rest upon his promise,
and to know, "Thus saith the Lord."

Refrain:
Jesus, Jesus, how I trust him!
How I've proved him o'er and o'er!
Jesus, Jesus, precious Jesus!
O for grace to trust him more!

O how sweet to trust in Jesus,
just to trust his cleansing blood;
and in simple faith to plunge me
neath the healing, cleansing flood!
(Refrain)

Yes, 'tis sweet to trust in Jesus,
just from sin and self to cease;
just from Jesus simply taking
life and rest, and joy and peace.
(Refrain)

I'm so glad I learned to trust thee,
precious Jesus, Savior, friend;
and I know that thou art with me,
wilt be with me to the end.
(Refrain)

Psalm 121:1-8

I lift up my eyes to the mountains—
  where does my help come from?
My help comes from the LORD,
  the Maker of heaven and earth.

He will not let your foot slip—
  he who watches over you will not slumber;
indeed, he who watches over Israel
  will neither slumber nor sleep.

The LORD watches over you—
  the LORD is your shade at your right hand;
the sun will not harm you by day,
  nor the moon by night.

The LORD will keep you from all harm—
  he will watch over your life;
the LORD will watch over your coming and going
  both now and forevermore.

The Gloria

Glory to the Father, and to the Son, and to the Holy Spirit: as
it was in the beginning, is now, and will be for ever. Amen.

2 Corinthians 5:17-18

Therefore, if anyone is in Christ, the new creation has come:
The old has gone, the new is here! All this is from God,
who reconciled us to himself through Christ and gave us the
ministry of reconciliation.

Silence
Lord, have mercy. Christ, have mercy. Lord, have mercy.

The Prayer of Our Lord

Our Father in heaven, hallowed be your Name,

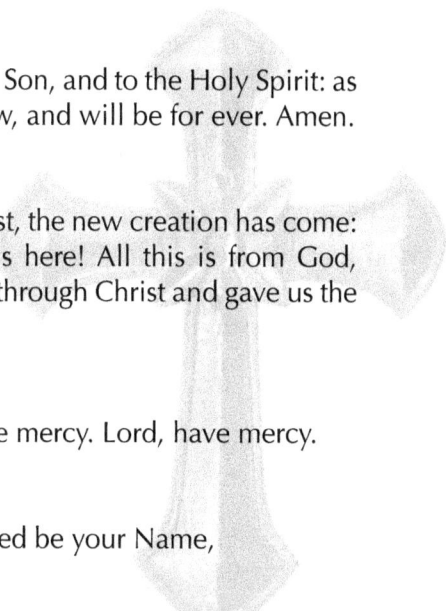

your kingdom come, your will be done,
on earth as it is in heaven.
Give us today our daily bread.
Forgive us our sins as we forgive those who sin against us.
Lead us not into temptation, but deliver us from evil.
For the kingdom, the power, and the glory are yours,
now and for ever. Amen.

A few moments of intercessory prayer
Lord, hear our prayer; And let our cry come to you.

Holy Day Prayer *(found on pages 131 to 158)*

Prayer for My City
Father God, I pray for the workers of Wyoming, that
they will work as though working for you. May they find
satisfaction in their work and receive fair pay. May they
work with honesty and integrity, knowing that you are the
ultimate provider and reward those who work hard and
do not pursue dishonest gain. Please grant them clarity of
mind and the physical strength necessary for their work. I
pray that managers and leaders will be aware that they are
ultimately accountable to you. Finally, I pray that you will
use all the work done by those in Wyoming for your purpose and glory. Amen.

Prayer for the Afternoon
Blessed Savior, at this hour you hung upon the cross,
stretching out your loving arms: Grant that all the peoples
of the earth may look to you and be saved; for your tender
mercies' sake. Amen.

Monday Evening

Philippians 1:2
Grace and peace to you from God our Father and the Lord
Jesus Christ.

The Jesus Creed
Love the Lord your God with all your heart and with all your
soul and with all your mind and with all your strength; and
love your neighbor as yourself.

Confession of Sin
Let us confess our sins against God and our neighbor.

Silence may be kept.

Most merciful God,
I confess that I have sinned against you
in thought, word, and deed,
by what I have done,
and by what I have left undone.
I have not loved you with my whole heart;
I have not loved my neighbor as myself.
I am truly sorry and I humbly repent.
For the sake of your Son Jesus Christ,
have mercy on me and forgive me;
that I may delight in your will,
and walk in your ways,
to the glory of your Name. Amen.

O God, make speed to save us; Lord, make haste to help us.

The Gloria
Glory to the Father, and to the Son, and to the Holy Spirit: as
it was in the beginning, is now, and will be for ever. Amen.

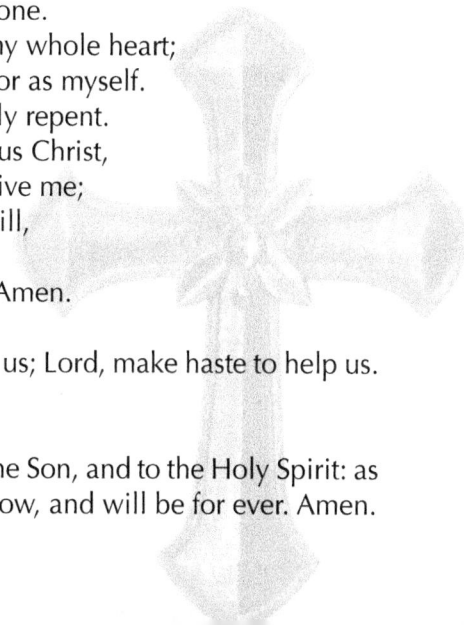

O Gracious Light
O gracious Light,
pure brightness of the everliving Father in heaven,
O Jesus Christ, holy and blessed!

Now as we come to the setting of the sun,
and our eyes behold the vesper light,
we sing your praises, O God: Father, Son, and Holy Spirit.

You are worthy at all times to be praised by happy voices,
O Son of God, O Giver of life,
and to be glorified through all the worlds.

The Evening Psalter—*Psalm 11*
In the LORD I take refuge.
  How then can you say to me:
  "Flee like a bird to your mountain.
For look, the wicked bend their bows;
  they set their arrows against the strings
to shoot from the shadows
  at the upright in heart.
When the foundations are being destroyed,
  what can the righteous do?"

The LORD is in his holy temple;
  the LORD is on his heavenly throne.
He observes everyone on earth;
  his eyes examine them.
The LORD examines the righteous,
  but the wicked, those who love violence,
  he hates with a passion.
On the wicked he will rain
  fiery coals and burning sulfur;
  a scorching wind will be their lot.

For the LORD is righteous,
  he loves justice;
  the upright will see his face.

The Gloria
Glory to the Father, and to the Son, and to the Holy Spirit: as it was in the beginning, is now, and will be for ever. Amen.

The Evening Lesson
New Testament Reading (found on pages 159 to 171)

The Apostles' Creed
I believe in God, the Father almighty,
Creator of heaven and earth.

I believe in Jesus Christ, his only Son, our Lord.
He was conceived by the power of the Holy Spirit
and born of the Virgin Mary.
He suffered under Pontius Pilate,
was crucified, died, and was buried.
He descended to the dead.
On the third day he rose again.
He ascended into heaven,
and is seated at the right hand of the Father.
He will come again to judge the living and the dead.

I believe in the Holy Spirit,
the holy catholic Church,
the communion of saints,
the forgiveness of sins,
the resurrection of the body,
and the life everlasting. Amen.

The Prayer of Our Lord
Our Father in heaven, hallowed be your Name,
your kingdom come, your will be done,

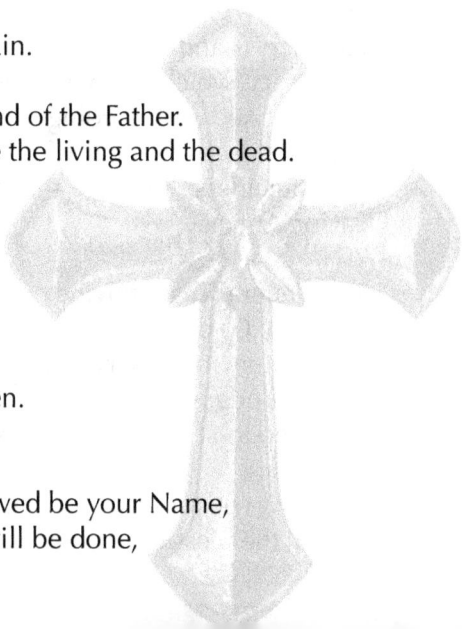

on earth as it is in heaven.
Give us today our daily bread.
Forgive us our sins as we forgive those who sin against us.
Lead us not into temptation, but deliver us from evil.
For the kingdom, the power, and the glory are yours,
now and for ever. Amen.

Prayer of Suffrage

Lord, we entreat you that this evening may be holy, good, and peaceful, that your holy angels may lead us in paths of peace and goodwill, that we may be pardoned and forgiven for our sins and offenses, that there may be peace to your Church and to the whole world, that we may depart this life in your faith and fear, and not be condemned before the great judgment seat of Christ, that we may be bound together by your Holy Spirit in the communion of all your saints, entrusting one another and all our life to Christ. To all of this we entreat you, Lord Christ.

Prayer for the Evening

Most holy God, the source of all good desires, all right judgments, and all just works: Give to us, your servants, that peace which the world cannot give, so that our minds may be fixed on the doing of your will, and that we, being delivered from the fear of all enemies, may live in peace and quietness; through the mercies of Christ Jesus our Savior. Amen.

The General Thanksgiving

Almighty God, Father of all mercies,
we your unworthy servants give you humble thanks
for all your goodness and loving kindness
to us and to all whom you have made.

We bless you for our creation, preservation,
and all the blessings of this life;

but above all for your immeasurable love
in the redemption of the world by our Lord Jesus Christ;
for the means of grace, and for the hope of glory.

And, we pray, give us such an awareness of your mercies,
that with truly thankful hearts we may show forth your
praise, not only with our lips, but in our lives,
by giving up our selves to your service,
and by walking before you
in holiness and righteousness all our days;
through Jesus Christ our Lord,
to whom, with you and the Holy Spirit,
be honor and glory throughout all ages. Amen.

Keep watch, dear Lord, with those who work, or watch, or
weep this night, and give your angels charge over those who
sleep. Tend the sick, Lord Christ; give rest to the weary, bless
the dying, soothe the suffering, pity the afflicted, shield the
joyous; and all for your love's sake. Amen.

Prayer for My City
Heavenly Father, it is your will that people should be at
peace with one another. But there are many in Wyoming
who would break that peace through criminal activity. I
ask, God, that you will restrain crime in the city. Protect
would-be victims of crime from experiencing violence. Heal
the scars, both physical and emotional, where violence has
already occurred. Act on behalf of the weak and oppose the
proud. I pray that you will confound the plans of gang leaders and protect young people from joining gangs. Please
provide the young men and women of Wyoming positive
mentors and role models and healthy alternatives to crime
and gangs. Replace any desire to do harm with a desire to
do good. Please make Wyoming safe for all. Amen.

Ephesians 3:20-21

Now to him who is able to do immeasurably more than all we ask or imagine, according to his power that is at work within us, to him be glory in the church and in Christ Jesus throughout all generations, for ever and ever! Amen.

Tuesday
Prayers

Tuesday Morning

Psalm 19:14
May these words of my mouth and this meditation of my heart be pleasing in your sight, LORD, my Rock and my Redeemer.

The Jesus Creed
Love the Lord your God with all your heart and with all your soul and with all your mind and with all your strength; and love your neighbor as yourself.

Confession of Sin
Let us confess our sins against God and our neighbor.

Silence may be kept.

Most merciful God,
I confess that I have sinned against you
in thought, word, and deed,
by what I have done,
and by what I have left undone.
I have not loved you with my whole heart;
I have not loved my neighbor as myself.
I am truly sorry and I humbly repent.
For the sake of your Son Jesus Christ,
have mercy on me and forgive me;
that I may delight in your will,
and walk in your ways,
to the glory of your Name. Amen.

Lord, open our lips. And our mouth shall proclaim your praise.

The Gloria
Glory to the Father, and to the Son, and to the Holy Spirit: as it was in the beginning, is now, and will be for ever. Amen.

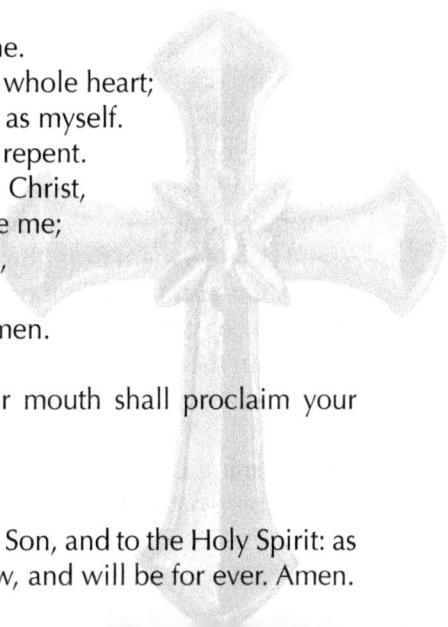

Worship the Lord in the beauty of holiness: Come let us adore him.

Psalter: Psalm 97

The LORD reigns, let the earth be glad;
  let the distant shores rejoice.
Clouds and thick darkness surround him;
  righteousness and justice are the foundation of his throne.
Fire goes before him
  and consumes his foes on every side.
His lightning lights up the world;
  the earth sees and trembles.
The mountains melt like wax before the LORD,
  before the Lord of all the earth.
The heavens proclaim his righteousness,
  and all peoples see his glory.
All who worship images are put to shame,
  those who boast in idols—
  worship him, all you gods!

Zion hears and rejoices
  and the villages of Judah are glad
  because of your judgments, LORD.
For you, LORD, are the Most High over all the earth;
  you are exalted far above all gods.
Let those who love the LORD hate evil,
  for he guards the lives of his faithful ones
  and delivers them from the hand of the wicked.
Light shines on the righteous
  and joy on the upright in heart.
Rejoice in the LORD, you who are righteous,
  and praise his holy name.

The Morning Lesson
Old Testament Reading (found on pages 159 to 171)

The Morning Song—*The Song of Moses (Ex. 15:1-6, 11-18)*
"I will sing to the LORD,
  for he is highly exalted.
Both horse and driver
  he has hurled into the sea.

"The LORD is my strength and my defense;
  he has become my salvation.
He is my God, and I will praise him,
  my father's God, and I will exalt him.
The LORD is a warrior;
  the LORD is his name.
Pharaoh's chariots and his army
  he has hurled into the sea.
The best of Pharaoh's officers
  are drowned in the Red Sea.
The deep waters have covered them;
  they sank to the depths like a stone.
Your right hand, LORD,
  was majestic in power.
Your right hand, LORD,
  shattered the enemy.

Who among the gods
  is like you, LORD?
Who is like you—
  majestic in holiness,
awesome in glory,
  working wonders?

"The LORD reigns for ever and ever."

The Apostles' Creed
I believe in God, the Father almighty,
Creator of heaven and earth.

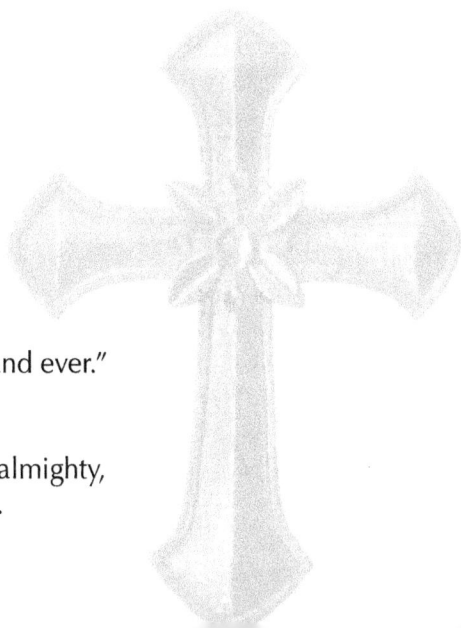

I believe in Jesus Christ, his only Son, our Lord.
He was conceived by the power of the Holy Spirit
and born of the Virgin Mary.
He suffered under Pontius Pilate,
was crucified, died, and was buried.
He descended to the dead.
On the third day he rose again.
He ascended into heaven,
and is seated at the right hand of the Father.
He will come again to judge the living and the dead.

I believe in the Holy Spirit,
the holy catholic Church,
the communion of saints,
the forgiveness of sins,
the resurrection of the body,
and the life everlasting. Amen.

The Prayer of Our Lord
Our Father in heaven, hallowed be your Name,
your kingdom come, your will be done,
on earth as it is in heaven.
Give us today our daily bread.
Forgive us our sins as we forgive those who sin against us.
Lead us not into temptation, but deliver us from evil.
For the kingdom, the power, and the glory are yours,
now and for ever. Amen.

Prayer for the Day
Heavenly Father, in you we live and move and have our
being: We humbly pray you so to guide and govern us by
your Holy Spirit, that in all the cares and occupations of our
life we may not forget you, but may remember that we are
ever walking in your sight; through Jesus Christ our Lord.
Amen.

Prayer for My City (Colossians 1:3-14)
Father God, I thank you for building up the Church in Wyoming. I praise you for rescuing us sinners from the dominion of darkness and for bringing us into the kingdom of your Son. Thank you for creating communities of faith, hope, and love. Thank you that through these local churches the gospel is going out and bearing fruit. I ask you to give the churches of Wyoming the knowledge of your will through the faithful teaching of your Word. I ask this so that believers living and serving in Wyoming will please you in every way and may have joy, endurance, and patience as they share your love with the world around them. Amen.

Ephesians 3:20-21
Now to him who is able to do immeasurably more than all we ask or imagine, according to his power that is at work within us, to him be glory in the church and in Christ Jesus throughout all generations, for ever and ever! Amen.

O God, make speed to save us; Lord, make haste to help us.

The Gloria
Glory to the Father, and to the Son, and to the Holy Spirit: as it was in the beginning, is now, and will be for ever. Amen.

Hymn Selection—*Come Thou Fount*
Come, Thou Fount of every blessing,
Tune my heart to sing Thy grace;
Streams of mercy, never ceasing,
Call for songs of loudest praise.

Teach me some melodious sonnet,
Sung by flaming tongues above.
Praise the mount! I'm fixed upon it,
Mount of Thy redeeming love.

Sorrowing I shall be in spirit,
Till released from flesh and sin,
Yet from what I do inherit,
Here Thy praises I'll begin;

Here I raise my Ebenezer;
Here by Thy great help I've come;
And I hope, by Thy good pleasure,
Safely to arrive at home.

Jesus sought me when a stranger,
Wandering from the fold of God;
He, to rescue me from danger,
Interposed His precious blood;

How His kindness yet pursues me
Mortal tongue can never tell,

Clothed in flesh, till death shall loose me
I cannot proclaim it well.

O to grace how great a debtor
Daily I'm constrained to be!
Let Thy goodness, like a fetter,
Bind my wandering heart to Thee.

Prone to wander, Lord, I feel it,
Prone to leave the God I love;
Here's my heart, O take and seal it,
Seal it for Thy courts above.

O that day when freed from sinning,
I shall see Thy lovely face;
Clothed then in blood washed linen
How I'll sing Thy sovereign grace;

Come, my Lord, no longer tarry,
Take my ransomed soul away;
Send thine angels now to carry
Me to realms of endless day.

Psalm 126:1-7

When the LORD restored the fortunes of Zion,
   we were like those who dreamed.
Our mouths were filled with laughter,
   our tongues with songs of joy.
Then it was said among the nations,
   "The LORD has done great things for them."
The LORD has done great things for us,
   and we are filled with joy.

Restore our fortunes, LORD,
   like streams in the Negev.
Those who sow with tears

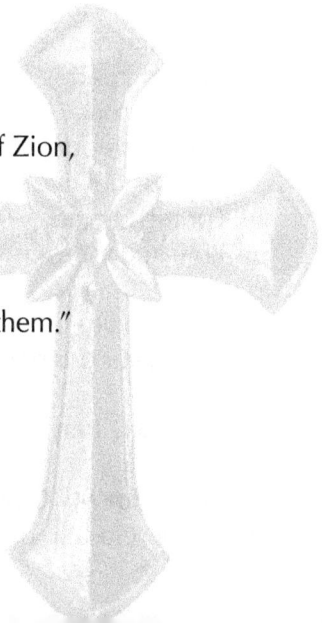

will reap with songs of joy.
Those who go out weeping,
   carrying seed to sow,
will return with songs of joy,
   carrying sheaves with them.

The Gloria
Glory to the Father, and to the Son, and to the Holy Spirit: as it was in the beginning, is now, and will be for ever. Amen.

Malachi 1:11
My name will be great among the nations, from where the sun rises to where it sets. In every place incense and pure offerings will be brought to me, because my name will be great among the nations," says the LORD Almighty.

Silence
Lord, have mercy. Christ, have mercy. Lord, have mercy.

The Prayer of Our Lord
Our Father in heaven, hallowed be your Name,
your kingdom come, your will be done,
on earth as it is in heaven.
Give us today our daily bread.
Forgive us our sins as we forgive those who sin against us.
Lead us not into temptation, but deliver us from evil.
For the kingdom, the power, and the glory are yours,
now and for ever. Amen.

A few moments of intercessory prayer
Lord, hear our prayer; And let our cry come to you.

Holy Day Prayer *(found on pages 131 to 158)*

Prayer for My City
Father God, I pray that city leaders will have wisdom

as they plan, rebuild, and repair the infrastructure of Wyoming. I pray that the roads, buildings, and utilities will create an environment that enables the people of Wyoming to work, rest, and enjoy the fruit of your creation. I pray that the parks will be safe places where families and individuals can come together to enjoy one another and the world you have made. I pray that the people of Wyoming will enjoy clean water, pure air, and an ordered environment. I pray that each person will do their part to create and maintain a beautiful city. Amen.

Prayer for the Afternoon
Almighty Savior, who at noonday called your servant Saint Paul to be an apostle to the Gentiles: We pray you to illumine the world with the radiance of your glory, that all nations may come and worship you; for you live and reign for ever and ever. Amen.

Tuesday Evening

Psalm 96:9
Worship the LORD in the splendor of his holiness; tremble before him, all the earth.

The Jesus Creed
Love the Lord your God with all your heart and with all your soul and with all your mind and with all your strength; and love your neighbor as yourself.

Confession of Sin
Let us confess our sins against God and our neighbor.

Silence may be kept.

Most merciful God,
I confess that I have sinned against you
in thought, word, and deed,
by what I have done,
and by what I have left undone.
I have not loved you with my whole heart;
I have not loved my neighbor as myself.
I am truly sorry and I humbly repent.
For the sake of your Son Jesus Christ,
have mercy on me and forgive me;
that I may delight in your will,
and walk in your ways,
to the glory of your Name. Amen.

O God, make speed to save us; Lord, make haste to help us.

The Gloria
Glory to the Father, and to the Son, and to the Holy Spirit: as it was in the beginning, is now, and will be for ever. Amen.

O Gracious Light
O gracious Light,
pure brightness of the everliving Father in heaven,
O Jesus Christ, holy and blessed!

Now as we come to the setting of the sun,
and our eyes behold the vesper light,
we sing your praises, O God: Father, Son, and Holy Spirit.

You are worthy at all times to be praised by happy voices,
O Son of God, O Giver of life,
and to be glorified through all the worlds.

The Evening Psalter—*Psalm 31:1-5, 15-17*
In you, LORD, I have taken refuge;
   let me never be put to shame;
   deliver me in your righteousness.
Turn your ear to me,
   come quickly to my rescue;
be my rock of refuge,
   a strong fortress to save me.
Since you are my rock and my fortress,
   for the sake of your name lead and guide me.
Keep me free from the trap that is set for me,
   for you are my refuge.
Into your hands I commit my spirit;
   deliver me, LORD, my faithful God.

My times are in your hands;
   deliver me from the hands of my enemies,
   from those who pursue me.
Let your face shine on your servant;
   save me in your unfailing love.
Let me not be put to shame, LORD,
   for I have cried out to you;
but let the wicked be put to shame
   and be silent in the realm of the dead.

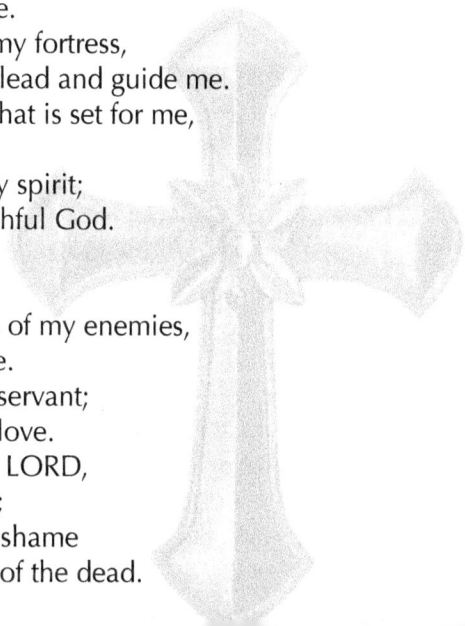

The Gloria
Glory to the Father, and to the Son, and to the Holy Spirit: as
it was in the beginning, is now, and will be for ever. Amen.

The Evening Lesson
New Testament Reading (found on pages 159 to 171)

The Apostles' Creed
I believe in God, the Father almighty,
Creator of heaven and earth.

I believe in Jesus Christ, his only Son, our Lord.
He was conceived by the power of the Holy Spirit
and born of the Virgin Mary.
He suffered under Pontius Pilate,
was crucified, died, and was buried.
He descended to the dead.
On the third day he rose again.
He ascended into heaven,
and is seated at the right hand of the Father.
He will come again to judge the living and the dead.

I believe in the Holy Spirit,
the holy catholic Church,
the communion of saints,
the forgiveness of sins,
the resurrection of the body,
and the life everlasting. Amen.

The Prayer of Our Lord
Our Father in heaven, hallowed be your Name,
your kingdom come, your will be done,
on earth as it is in heaven.
Give us today our daily bread.
Forgive us our sins as we forgive those who sin against us.
Lead us not into temptation, but deliver us from evil.

For the kingdom, the power, and the glory are yours,
now and for ever. Amen.

Prayer of Suffrage
Show us your mercy, O Lord;
And grant us your salvation.
Clothe your ministers with righteousness;
Let your people sing with joy.
Give peace, O Lord, in all the world;
For only in you can we live in safety.
Lord, keep this nation under your care;
And guide us in the way of justice and truth.
Let your way be known upon earth;
Your saving health among all nations.
Let not the needy, O Lord, be forgotten;
Nor the hope of the poor be taken away.
Create in us clean hearts, O God;
And sustain us with your Holy Spirit.

Prayer for the Evening
Be our light in the darkness, O Lord, and in your great mercy defend us from all perils and dangers of this night; for the love of your only Son, our Savior Jesus Christ. Amen.

The General Thanksgiving
Almighty God, Father of all mercies,
we your unworthy servants give you humble thanks
for all your goodness and loving kindness
to us and to all whom you have made.

We bless you for our creation, preservation,
and all the blessings of this life;
but above all for your immeasurable love
in the redemption of the world by our Lord Jesus Christ;
for the means of grace, and for the hope of glory.

And, we pray, give us such an awareness of your mercies,
that with truly thankful hearts we may show forth your
praise, not only with our lips, but in our lives,
by giving up our selves to your service,
and by walking before you
in holiness and righteousness all our days;
through Jesus Christ our Lord,
to whom, with you and the Holy Spirit,
be honor and glory throughout all ages. Amen.

O God and Father of all, whom the whole heavens adore:
Let the whole earth also worship you, all nations obey you,
all tongues confess and bless you, and men and women
everywhere love you and serve you in peace; through Jesus
Christ our Lord. Amen.

Prayer for My City
Father God, I pray for students across the city of Wyoming.
I pray that they will be diligent in their work and that they
will see the value of their education. I pray that you will
grant the students clear minds in their studies. I pray that the
schools will be safe places for all students to learn and make
friends. I pray that students will be able to resist negative
peer pressure and the temptations of youthful desires. I pray
that believing students will be salt and light, as they serve
as examples to others of hard work, kindness, and respect. I
pray that they will be faithful witnesses for you. Amen.

Romans 15:13
May the God of hope fill you with all joy and peace as you
trust in him, so that you may overflow with hope by the
power of the Holy Spirit. Amen.

WEDNESDAY
PRAYERS

Psalm 43:3
Send out your light and your truth, that they may lead me, and bring me to your holy hill and to your dwelling.

The Jesus Creed
Love the Lord your God with all your heart and with all your soul and with all your mind and with all your strength; and love your neighbor as yourself.

Confession of Sin
Let us confess our sins against God and our neighbor.

Silence may be kept.

Most merciful God,
I confess that I have sinned against you
in thought, word, and deed,
by what I have done,
and by what I have left undone.
I have not loved you with my whole heart;
I have not loved my neighbor as myself.
I am truly sorry and I humbly repent.
For the sake of your Son Jesus Christ,
have mercy on me and forgive me;
that I may delight in your will,
and walk in your ways,
to the glory of your Name. Amen.

Lord, open our lips. And our mouth shall proclaim your praise.

The Gloria
Glory to the Father, and to the Son, and to the Holy Spirit: as it was in the beginning, is now, and will be for ever. Amen.

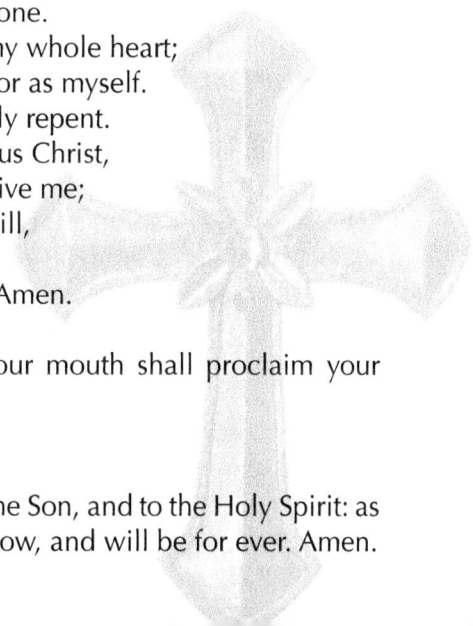

Worship the Lord in the beauty of holiness: Come let us
adore him.

Jubilate—*Psalm 100*
Shout for joy to the LORD, all the earth.
Worship the LORD with gladness;
    come before him with joyful songs.
Know that the LORD is God.
    It is he who made us, and we are his;
    we are his people, the sheep of his pasture.

Enter his gates with thanksgiving
    and his courts with praise;
    give thanks to him and praise his name.
For the LORD is good and his love endures forever;
    his faithfulness continues through all generations.

The Gloria
Glory to the Father, and to the Son, and to the Holy Spirit: as
it was in the beginning, is now, and will be for ever. Amen.

The Morning Lesson
Old Testament Reading (found on pages 159 to 171)

The Morning Song—*The Song of Zechariah (Lk. 1:68-79)*
"Praise be to the Lord, the God of Israel,
    because he has come to his people and redeemed them.
He has raised up a horn of salvation for us
    in the house of his servant David
(as he said through his holy prophets of long ago),
salvation from our enemies
    and from the hand of all who hate us—
to show mercy to our ancestors
    and to remember his holy covenant,
 the oath he swore to our father Abraham:
to rescue us from the hand of our enemies,

and to enable us to serve him without fear
in holiness and righteousness before him all our days.
And you, my child, will be called a prophet of the Most
High;
for you will go on before the Lord to prepare the way for
him, to give his people the knowledge of salvation
through the forgiveness of their sins,
because of the tender mercy of our God,
by which the rising sun will come to us from heaven
to shine on those living in darkness
and in the shadow of death,
to guide our feet into the path of peace."

The Apostles' Creed
I believe in God, the Father almighty,
Creator of heaven and earth.

I believe in Jesus Christ, his only Son, our Lord.
He was conceived by the power of the Holy Spirit
and born of the Virgin Mary.
He suffered under Pontius Pilate,
was crucified, died, and was buried.
He descended to the dead.
On the third day he rose again.
He ascended into heaven,
and is seated at the right hand of the Father.
He will come again to judge the living and the dead.

I believe in the Holy Spirit,
the holy catholic Church,
the communion of saints,
the forgiveness of sins,
the resurrection of the body,
and the life everlasting. Amen.

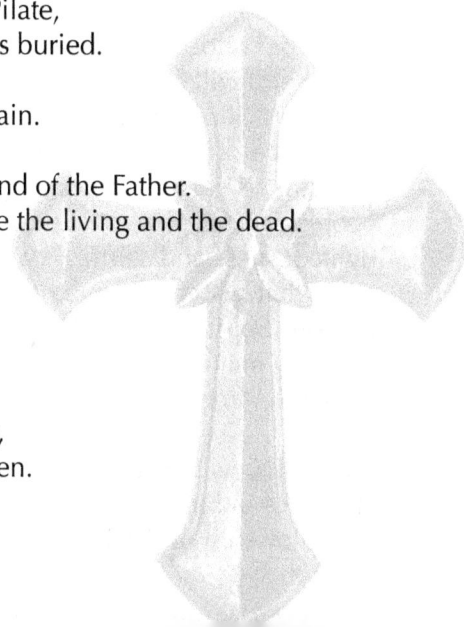

The Prayer of Our Lord
Our Father in heaven, hallowed be your Name,
your kingdom come, your will be done,
on earth as it is in heaven.
Give us today our daily bread.
Forgive us our sins as we forgive those who sin against us.
Lead us not into temptation, but deliver us from evil.
For the kingdom, the power, and the glory are yours,
now and for ever. Amen.

Prayer for the Day
O God, the King eternal, whose light divides the day from
the night and turns the shadow of death into the morning:
Drive far from us all wrong desires, incline our hearts to
keep your law, and guide our feet into the way of peace;
that, having done your will with cheerfulness during the
day, we may, when night comes, rejoice to give you thanks;
through Jesus Christ our Lord. Amen.

Prayer for My City (John 16:5-16)
Father God, I thank you for sending your Holy Spirit into
the world and into the city of Wyoming. I pray that your
Holy Spirit will convict the world of sin, righteousness, and
judgment. Show us our sin, that our sin brings guilt, and that
the prince of this world already stands condemned. Spirit
of truth, reveal the will of the Father and the Son to the
people of Wyoming. Shake the complacent from their self-
righteousness and spiritual darkness. Shine your light upon
us so that we can see you for who you really are. Father,
by your Spirit, point the people of Wyoming to Christ so
that they may find healing, comfort, and hope in your great
salvation. Amen.

2 Corinthians 13:14
The grace of our Lord Jesus Christ, and the love of God, and
the fellowship of the Holy Spirit, be with us all evermore.
Amen.

Wednesday Afternoon

O God, make speed to save us; Lord, make haste to help us.

The Gloria
Glory to the Father, and to the Son, and to the Holy Spirit: as it was in the beginning, is now, and will be for ever. Amen.

Hymn Selection—*It Is Well With My Soul*
When peace, like a river, attendeth my way,
When sorrows like sea billows roll;
Whatever my lot, Thou has taught me to say,
It is well, it is well, with my soul.

Refrain:
It is well, with my soul,
It is well, with my soul,
It is well, It is well, with my soul,

Though Satan should buffet, though trials should come,
Let this blest assurance control,
That Christ has regarded my helpless estate,
And hath shed His own blood for my soul.
(Refrain)

My sin, oh, the bliss of this glorious thought!
My sin, not in part but the whole,
Is nailed to the cross, and I bear it no more,
Praise the Lord, praise the Lord, O my soul!
(Refrain)

For me, be it Christ, be it Christ hence to live:
If Jordan above me shall roll,
No pang shall be mine, for in death as in life
Thou wilt whisper Thy peace to my soul.
(Refrain)

But, Lord, 'tis for Thee, for Thy coming we wait,
The sky, not the grave, is our goal;
Oh trump of the angel! Oh voice of the Lord!
Blessed hope, blessed rest of my soul!
(Refrain)

And Lord, haste the day when my faith shall be sight,
The clouds be rolled back as a scroll;
The trump shall resound, and the Lord shall descend,
Even so, it is well with my soul.
(Refrain)

Psalm 19

The heavens declare the glory of God;
   the skies proclaim the work of his hands.
Day after day they pour forth speech;
   night after night they reveal knowledge.
They have no speech, they use no words;
   no sound is heard from them.
Yet their voice goes out into all the earth,
   their words to the ends of the world.
In the heavens God has pitched a tent for the sun.
It is like a bridegroom coming out of his chamber,
   like a champion rejoicing to run his course.
It rises at one end of the heavens
   and makes its circuit to the other;
   nothing is deprived of its warmth.

The law of the LORD is perfect,
   refreshing the soul.
The statutes of the LORD are trustworthy,
   making wise the simple.
The precepts of the LORD are right,
   giving joy to the heart.
The commands of the LORD are radiant,
   giving light to the eyes.

The fear of the LORD is pure,
   enduring forever.
The decrees of the LORD are firm,
   and all of them are righteous.

 They are more precious than gold,
   than much pure gold;
they are sweeter than honey,
   than honey from the honeycomb.
By them your servant is warned;
   in keeping them there is great reward.
But who can discern their own errors?
   Forgive my hidden faults.
Keep your servant also from willful sins;
   may they not rule over me.
Then I will be blameless,
   innocent of great transgression.

May these words of my mouth and this meditation of my
heart
   be pleasing in your sight,
   LORD, my Rock and my Redeemer.

The Gloria
Glory to the Father, and to the Son, and to the Holy Spirit: as
it was in the beginning, is now, and will be for ever. Amen.

Romans 8:1-3
Therefore, there is now no condemnation for those who are
in Christ Jesus, because through Christ Jesus the law of the
Spirit of life set me free from the law of sin and death. For
what the law was powerless to do in that it was weakened
by the sinful nature, God did by sending his own Son in the
likeness of sinful man to be a sin offering.

Silence

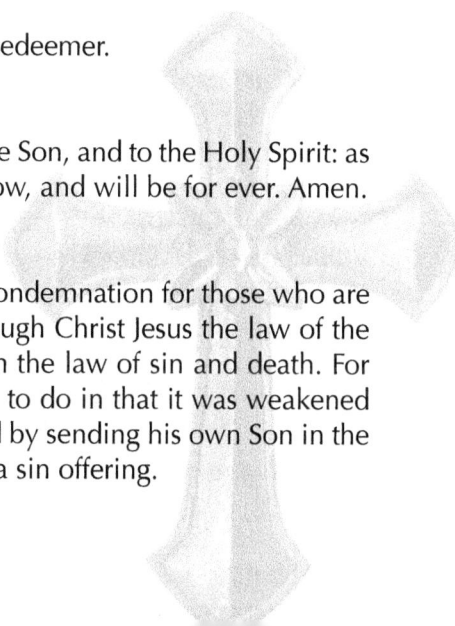

Lord, have mercy. Christ, have mercy. Lord, have mercy.

The Prayer of Our Lord
Our Father in heaven, hallowed be your Name,
your kingdom come, your will be done,
on earth as it is in heaven.
Give us today our daily bread.
Forgive us our sins as we forgive those who sin against us.
Lead us not into temptation, but deliver us from evil.
For the kingdom, the power, and the glory are yours,
now and for ever. Amen.

A few moments of intercessory prayer
Lord, hear our prayer; And let our cry come to you.

Holy Day Prayer *(found on pages 131 to 158)*

Prayer for My City
Heavenly Father, all authority comes from you. In your wisdom, you have established leaders with governing authority in the city of Wyoming. I pray especially for those public servants who have the task to hold back crime, uphold the cause of justice, defend the weak, and protect public safety. I pray for the police and judges, that they will hold no terror for those who do right, but bring just punishment on those who do evil. Give them wisdom, a spirit of justice, and safety from harm. I also thank you for others in public safety: for firefighters and paramedics, who risk their lives for the safety of others. Grant them safety as they serve Wyoming. Amen.

Prayer for the Afternoon
Lord Jesus Christ, you said to your apostles, "Peace I give to you; my own peace I leave with you:" Regard not our sins, but the faith of your Church, and give to us the peace and unity of that heavenly City, where with the Father and the Holy Spirit you live and reign, now and for ever. Amen.

Wednesday Evening

Psalm 74:15,16
It was you who opened up springs and streams; you dried up the ever-flowing rivers. The day is yours, and yours also the night; you established the sun and moon.

The Jesus Creed
Love the Lord your God with all your heart and with all your soul and with all your mind and with all your strength; and love your neighbor as yourself.

Confession of Sin
Let us confess our sins against God and our neighbor.

Silence may be kept.

Most merciful God,
I confess that I have sinned against you
in thought, word, and deed,
by what I have done,
and by what I have left undone.
I have not loved you with my whole heart;
I have not loved my neighbor as myself.
I am truly sorry and I humbly repent.
For the sake of your Son Jesus Christ,
have mercy on me and forgive me;
that I may delight in your will,
and walk in your ways,
to the glory of your Name. Amen.

O God, make speed to save us; Lord, make haste to help us.

The Gloria
Glory to the Father, and to the Son, and to the Holy Spirit: as it was in the beginning, is now, and will be for ever. Amen.

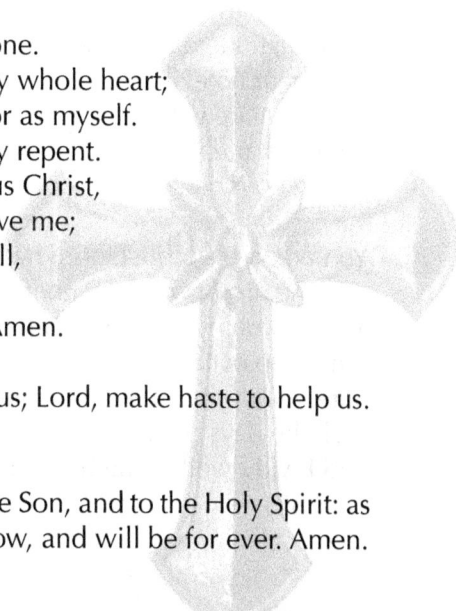

O Gracious Light
O gracious Light,
pure brightness of the everliving Father in heaven,
O Jesus Christ, holy and blessed!

Now as we come to the setting of the sun,
and our eyes behold the vesper light,
we sing your praises, O God: Father, Son, and Holy Spirit.

You are worthy at all times to be praised by happy voices,
O Son of God, O Giver of life,
and to be glorified through all the worlds.

The Evening Psalter—*Psalm 23*
The LORD is my shepherd, I lack nothing.
He makes me lie down in green pastures,
he leads me beside quiet waters,
    he refreshes my soul.
He guides me along the right paths
    for his name's sake.
Even though I walk
    through the darkest valley,
I will fear no evil,
    for you are with me;
your rod and your staff,
    they comfort me.

You prepare a table before me
    in the presence of my enemies.
You anoint my head with oil;
    my cup overflows.
Surely your goodness and love will follow me
    all the days of my life,
and I will dwell in the house of the LORD
    forever.

The Gloria
Glory to the Father, and to the Son, and to the Holy Spirit: as it was in the beginning, is now, and will be for ever. Amen.

The Evening Lesson
New Testament Reading (found on pages 159 to 171)

The Apostles' Creed
I believe in God, the Father almighty,
Creator of heaven and earth.

I believe in Jesus Christ, his only Son, our Lord.
He was conceived by the power of the Holy Spirit
and born of the Virgin Mary.
He suffered under Pontius Pilate,
was crucified, died, and was buried.
He descended to the dead.
On the third day he rose again.
He ascended into heaven,
and is seated at the right hand of the Father.
He will come again to judge the living and the dead.

I believe in the Holy Spirit,
the holy catholic Church,
the communion of saints,
the forgiveness of sins,
the resurrection of the body,
and the life everlasting. Amen.

The Prayer of Our Lord
Our Father in heaven, hallowed be your Name,
your kingdom come, your will be done,
on earth as it is in heaven.
Give us today our daily bread.
Forgive us our sins as we forgive those who sin against us.
Lead us not into temptation, but deliver us from evil.

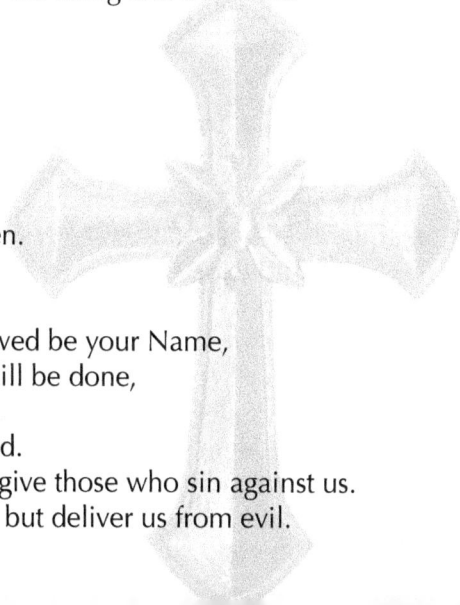

For the kingdom, the power, and the glory are yours,
now and for ever. Amen.

Prayer of Suffrage

Lord, we entreat you that this evening may be holy, good, and peaceful, that your holy angels may lead us in paths of peace and goodwill, that we may be pardoned and forgiven for our sins and offenses, that there may be peace to your Church and to the whole world, that we may depart this life in your faith and fear, and not be condemned before the great judgment seat of Christ, that we may be bound together by your Holy Spirit in the communion of all your saints, entrusting one another and all our life to Christ. To all of this we entreat you, Lord Christ.

Prayer for the Evening

O God, the life of all who live, the light of the faithful, the strength of those who labor, and the repose of the dead: We thank you for the blessings of the day that is past, and humbly ask for your protection through the coming night. Bring us in safety to the morning hours; through him who died and rose again for us, your Son our Savior Jesus Christ. Amen.

The General Thanksgiving

Almighty God, Father of all mercies,
we your unworthy servants give you humble thanks
for all your goodness and loving kindness
to us and to all whom you have made.

We bless you for our creation, preservation,
and all the blessings of this life;
but above all for your immeasurable love
in the redemption of the world by our Lord Jesus Christ;
for the means of grace, and for the hope of glory.

And, we pray, give us such an awareness of your mercies,
that with truly thankful hearts we may show forth your
praise, not only with our lips, but in our lives,
by giving up our selves to your service,
and by walking before you
in holiness and righteousness all our days;
through Jesus Christ our Lord,
to whom, with you and the Holy Spirit,
be honor and glory throughout all ages. Amen.

O God, you manifest in your servants the signs of your
presence: Send forth upon us the Spirit of love, that in
companionship with one another your abounding grace
may increase among us; through Jesus Christ our Lord.
Amen.

Prayer for My City
Father of all, you have made all people in this world, all
people of Wyoming, in your image. I pray that you will
break down walls of discrimination, whether they are based
on race, class, economic status, or gender. I pray that the
people of Wyoming will see one another as precious and
loved by you. I pray that the Church of Wyoming will be a
beacon of love and reconciliation. Give us a vision, Lord,
for what it really means to love our neighbors as you love
the world. Lord, I look forward to the day when people from
every nation, tongue, and tribe will worship you together.
Amen.

2 Corinthians 13:14
The grace of our Lord Jesus Christ, and the love of God, and
the fellowship of the Holy Spirit, be with us all evermore.
Amen.

THURSDAY
PRAYERS

Thursday Morning

Habakkuk 2:20
The LORD is in his holy temple; let all the earth be silent before him.

The Jesus Creed
Love the Lord your God with all your heart and with all your soul and with all your mind and with all your strength; and love your neighbor as yourself.

Confession of Sin
Let us confess our sins against God and our neighbor.

Silence may be kept.

Most merciful God,
I confess that I have sinned against you
in thought, word, and deed,
by what I have done,
and by what I have left undone.
I have not loved you with my whole heart;
I have not loved my neighbor as myself.
I am truly sorry and I humbly repent.
For the sake of your Son Jesus Christ,
have mercy on me and forgive me;
that I may delight in your will,
and walk in your ways,
to the glory of your Name. Amen.

Lord, open our lips. And our mouth shall proclaim your praise.

The Gloria
Glory to the Father, and to the Son, and to the Holy Spirit: as it was in the beginning, is now, and will be for ever. Amen.

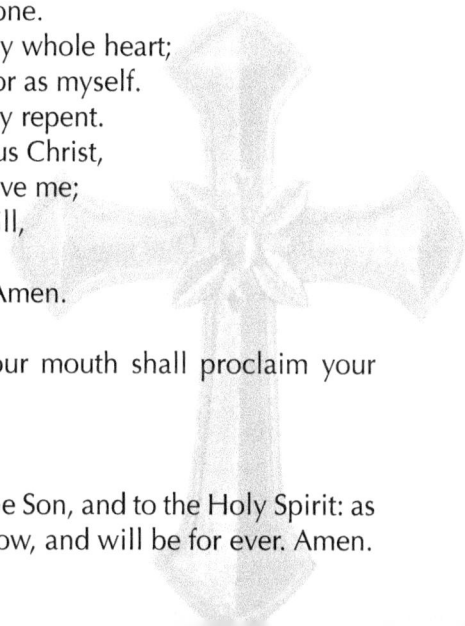

Worship the Lord in the beauty of holiness: Come let us adore him.

Venite—*Psalm 95*
Come, let us sing for joy to the LORD;
   let us shout aloud to the Rock of our salvation.
Let us come before him with thanksgiving
   and extol him with music and song.
For the LORD is the great God,
   the great King above all gods.
In his hand are the depths of the earth,
   and the mountain peaks belong to him.
The sea is his, for he made it,
   and his hands formed the dry land.

Come, let us bow down in worship,
   let us kneel before the LORD our Maker;
for he is our God
   and we are the people of his pasture,
   the flock under his care.

Today, if only you would hear his voice,
"Do not harden your hearts as you did at Meribah,
   as you did that day at Massah in the wilderness,
where your ancestors tested me;
   they tried me, though they had seen what I did.
For forty years I was angry with that generation;
   I said, 'They are a people whose hearts go astray,
   and they have not known my ways.'
So I declared on oath in my anger,
   'They shall never enter my rest.'"

The Gloria
Glory to the Father, and to the Son, and to the Holy Spirit: as it was in the beginning, is now, and will be for ever. Amen.

The Morning Lesson
Old Testament Reading (found on pages 159 to 171)

The Morning Song—*The Song of Mary (Luke 1:46-55)*
And Mary said:
   "My soul glorifies the Lord
and my spirit rejoices in God my Savior,
for he has been mindful
   of the humble state of his servant.
From now on all generations will call me blessed,
for the Mighty One has done great things for me—
   holy is his name.
His mercy extends to those who fear him,
   from generation to generation.
He has performed mighty deeds with his arm;
   he has scattered those who are proud in their inmost
thoughts.
He has brought down rulers from their thrones
   but has lifted up the humble.
He has filled the hungry with good things
   but has sent the rich away empty.
He has helped his servant Israel,
   remembering to be merciful
to Abraham and his descendants forever,
   just as he promised our ancestors."

The Apostles' Creed
I believe in God, the Father almighty,
Creator of heaven and earth.

I believe in Jesus Christ, his only Son, our Lord.
He was conceived by the power of the Holy Spirit
and born of the Virgin Mary.
He suffered under Pontius Pilate,
was crucified, died, and was buried.
He descended to the dead.

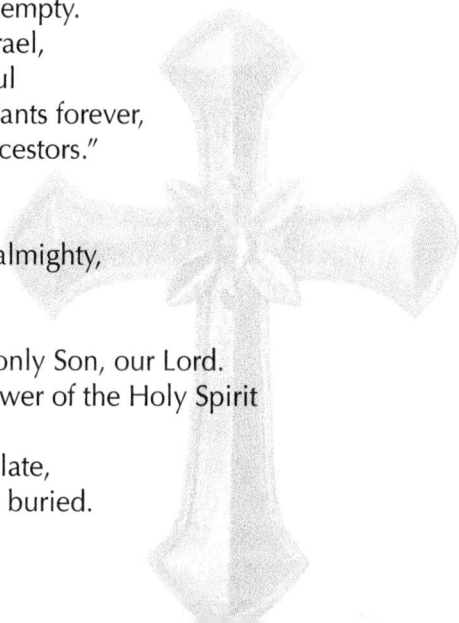

On the third day he rose again.
He ascended into heaven,
and is seated at the right hand of the Father.
He will come again to judge the living and the dead.

I believe in the Holy Spirit,
the holy catholic Church,
the communion of saints,
the forgiveness of sins,
the resurrection of the body,
and the life everlasting. Amen.

The Prayer of Our Lord
Our Father in heaven, hallowed be your Name,
your kingdom come, your will be done,
on earth as it is in heaven.
Give us today our daily bread.
Forgive us our sins as we forgive those who sin against us.
Lead us not into temptation, but deliver us from evil.
For the kingdom, the power, and the glory are yours,
now and for ever. Amen.

Prayer for the Day
O God, the author of peace and lover of concord, to know you is eternal life and to serve you is perfect freedom: Defend us, your humble servants, in all assaults of our enemies; that we, surely trusting in your defense, may not fear the power of any adversaries; through the might of Jesus Christ our Lord. Amen.

Prayer for My City (Matthew 9:35-10:42)
Father God, I pray that you will send your witnesses into Wyoming. Raise up individuals who will make your name great in Wyoming, who will proclaim the nearness of your kingdom, and who will demonstrate your presence by their deeds. Give them the words to speak, as though the

Spirit were speaking through them. Grant them success. But, when they encounter opposition, teach them to fear you, our God, and not man. I also pray that as your followers go to work, spend time with their families, and fellowship with their friends and neighbors, they will act as salt and light in the city of Wyoming. Amen.

Romans 15:13
May the God of hope fill you with all joy and peace as you trust in him, so that you may overflow with hope by the power of the Holy Spirit. Amen.

Thursday Afternoon

O God, make speed to save us; Lord, make haste to help us.

The Gloria
Glory to the Father, and to the Son, and to the Holy Spirit: as it was in the beginning, is now, and will be for ever. Amen.

Hymn Selection—*Be Thou My Vision*
Be Thou my Vision, O Lord of my heart;
Naught be all else to me, save that Thou art.
Thou my best Thought, by day or by night,
Waking or sleeping, Thy presence my light.

Be Thou my Wisdom, and Thou my true Word;
I ever with Thee and Thou with me, Lord;
Thou my great Father, I Thy true son;
Thou in me dwelling, and I with Thee one.

Be Thou my battle Shield, Sword for the fight;
Be Thou my Dignity, Thou my Delight;
Thou my soul's Shelter, Thou my high Tower:
Raise Thou me heavenward, O Power of my power.

Riches I heed not, nor man's empty praise,
Thou mine Inheritance, now and always:
Thou and Thou only, first in my heart,
High King of Heaven, my Treasure Thou art.

High King of Heaven, my victory won,
May I reach Heaven's joys, O bright Heaven's Sun!
Heart of my own heart, whatever befall,
Still be my Vision, O Ruler of all.

Psalm 67
May God be gracious to us and bless us

and make his face shine on us—
so that your ways may be known on earth,
    your salvation among all nations.

May the peoples praise you, God;
    may all the peoples praise you.
May the nations be glad and sing for joy,
    for you rule the peoples with equity
    and guide the nations of the earth.
May the peoples praise you, God;
    may all the peoples praise you.

The land yields its harvest;
    God, our God, blesses us.
May God bless us still,
    so that all the ends of the earth will fear him.

The Gloria
Glory to the Father, and to the Son, and to the Holy Spirit: *
as it was in the beginning, is now, and will be for ever.
Amen.

John 3:16-17
For God so loved the world that he gave his one and only
Son, that whoever believes in him shall not perish but have
eternal life. For God did not send his Son into the world to
condemn the world, but to save the world through him.

Silence
Lord, have mercy. Christ, have mercy. Lord, have mercy.

The Prayer of Our Lord
Our Father in heaven, hallowed be your Name,
your kingdom come, your will be done,
on earth as it is in heaven.
Give us today our daily bread.

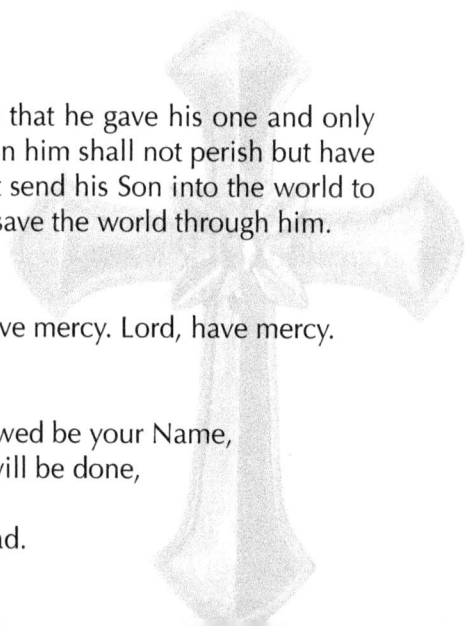

Forgive us our sins as we forgive those who sin against us.
Lead us not into temptation, but deliver us from evil.
For the kingdom, the power, and the glory are yours,
now and for ever. Amen.

A few moments of intercessory prayer
Lord, hear our prayer; And let our cry come to you.

Holy Day Prayer *(found on pages 131 to 158)*

Prayer for My City
Father, you are the God of all wisdom, knowledge, and
truth. I pray for schools in the city of Wyoming. I pray for
the school administrators, the principals, the teachers, and
all those who work in the school system. May the schools
of Wyoming help to prepare students for adult lives that
will bring honor and glory to you. I pray that you will provide resources to the schools in Wyoming and that you will
help key decision makers to wisely steward those resources
entrusted to them, and to be able to navigate the many
changes and challenges they face. Amen.

Prayer for the Afternoon
Almighty God, kindle, we pray, in every heart the true love
of peace, and guide with your wisdom those who take
counsel for the nations of the earth, that in tranquillity your
dominion may increase until the earth is filled with the
knowledge of your love; through Jesus Christ our Lord, who
lives and reigns with you, in the unity of the Holy Spirit, one
God, now and for ever. Amen.

Thursday Evening

Psalm 16:7-8
I will praise the LORD, who counsels me; even at night my heart instructs me. I keep my eyes always on the LORD. With him at my right hand, I will not be shaken.

The Jesus Creed
Love the Lord your God with all your heart and with all your soul and with all your mind and with all your strength; and love your neighbor as yourself.

Confession of Sin
Let us confess our sins against God and our neighbor.

Silence may be kept.

Most merciful God,
I confess that I have sinned against you
in thought, word, and deed,
by what I have done,
and by what I have left undone.
I have not loved you with my whole heart;
I have not loved my neighbor as myself.
I am truly sorry and I humbly repent.
For the sake of your Son Jesus Christ,
have mercy on me and forgive me;
that I may delight in your will,
and walk in your ways,
to the glory of your Name. Amen.

O God, make speed to save us; Lord, make haste to help us.

The Gloria
Glory to the Father, and to the Son, and to the Holy Spirit: as it was in the beginning, is now, and will be for ever. Amen.

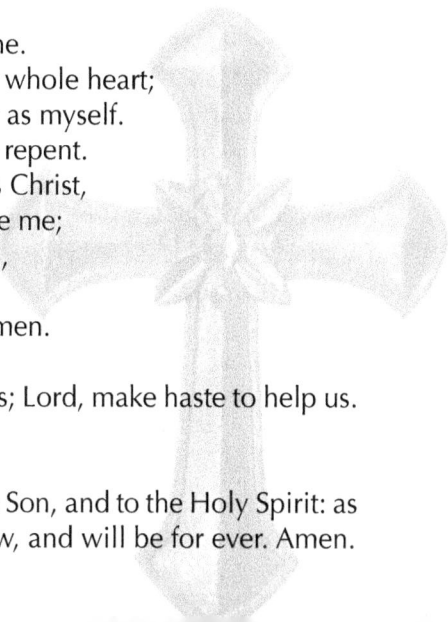

O Gracious Light
O gracious Light,
pure brightness of the everliving Father in heaven,
O Jesus Christ, holy and blessed!

Now as we come to the setting of the sun,
and our eyes behold the vesper light,
we sing your praises, O God: Father, Son, and Holy Spirit.

You are worthy at all times to be praised by happy voices,
O Son of God, O Giver of life,
and to be glorified through all the worlds.

The Evening Psalter—*Psalm 42:1-7*
As the deer pants for streams of water,
   so my soul pants for you, my God.
My soul thirsts for God, for the living God.
   When can I go and meet with God?
My tears have been my food
   day and night,
while people say to me all day long,
   "Where is your God?"
These things I remember
   as I pour out my soul:
how I used to go to the house of God
   under the protection of the Mighty One
with shouts of joy and praise
   among the festive throng.

Why, my soul, are you downcast?
   Why so disturbed within me?
Put your hope in God,
   for I will yet praise him,
   my Savior and my God.

My soul is downcast within me;

therefore I will remember you
from the land of the Jordan,
   the heights of Hermon—from Mount Mizar.
Deep calls to deep
   in the roar of your waterfalls;
all your waves and breakers
   have swept over me.

The Gloria
Glory to the Father, and to the Son, and to the Holy Spirit: as
it was in the beginning, is now, and will be for ever. Amen.

The Evening Lesson
New Testament Reading (found on pages 159 to 171)

The Apostles' Creed
I believe in God, the Father almighty,
Creator of heaven and earth.

I believe in Jesus Christ, his only Son, our Lord.
He was conceived by the power of the Holy Spirit
and born of the Virgin Mary.
He suffered under Pontius Pilate,
was crucified, died, and was buried.
He descended to the dead.
On the third day he rose again.
He ascended into heaven,
and is seated at the right hand of the Father.
He will come again to judge the living and the dead.

I believe in the Holy Spirit,
the holy catholic Church,
the communion of saints,
the forgiveness of sins,
the resurrection of the body,
and the life everlasting. Amen.

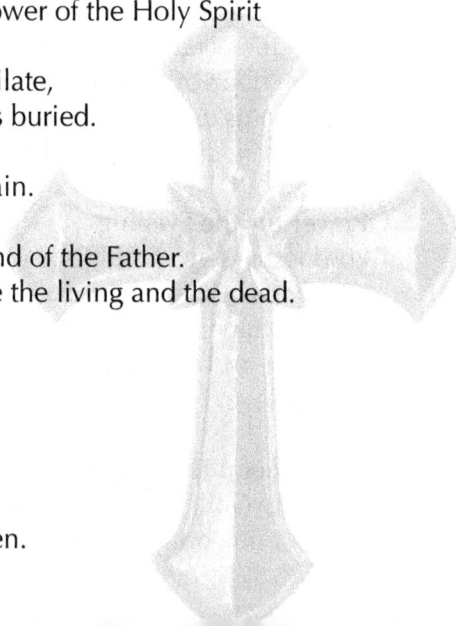

The Prayer of Our Lord

Our Father in heaven, hallowed be your Name,
your kingdom come, your will be done,
on earth as it is in heaven.
Give us today our daily bread.
Forgive us our sins as we forgive those who sin against us.
Lead us not into temptation, but deliver us from evil.
For the kingdom, the power, and the glory are yours,
now and for ever. Amen.

Prayer of Suffrage

Show us your mercy, O Lord;
And grant us your salvation.
Clothe your ministers with righteousness;
Let your people sing with joy.
Give peace, O Lord, in all the world;
For only in you can we live in safety
Lord, keep this nation under your care;
And guide us in the way of justice and truth.
Let your way be known upon earth;
Your saving health among all nations.
Let not the needy, O Lord, be forgotten;
Nor the hope of the poor be taken away.
Create in us clean hearts, O God;
And sustain us with your Holy Spirit.

Prayer for the Evening

Lord Jesus, stay with us, for evening is at hand and the day
is past; be our companion in the way, kindle our hearts, and
awaken hope, that we may know you as you are revealed in
Scripture and the breaking of bread. Grant this for the sake
of your love. Amen.

The General Thanksgiving

Almighty God, Father of all mercies,
we your unworthy servants give you humble thanks

for all your goodness and loving kindness
to us and to all whom you have made.
We bless you for our creation, preservation,
and all the blessings of this life;
but above all for your immeasurable love
in the redemption of the world by our Lord Jesus Christ;
for the means of grace, and for the hope of glory.

And, we pray, give us such an awareness of your mercies,
that with truly thankful hearts we may show forth your
praise, not only with our lips, but in our lives,
by giving up our selves to your service,
and by walking before you
in holiness and righteousness all our days;
through Jesus Christ our Lord,
to whom, with you and the Holy Spirit,
be honor and glory throughout all ages. Amen.

O God and Father of all, whom the whole heavens adore:
Let the whole earth also worship you, all nations obey you,
all tongues confess and bless you, and men and women
everywhere love you and serve you in peace; through Jesus
Christ our Lord. Amen.

Prayer for My City
Heavenly Father, I pray for the elderly in Wyoming. I pray for
their health, that you will demonstrate your healing power
in their lives for your glory. I pray for their minds, that you
will give them clarity of thought. I pray that you will give
them rest, contentment, and joy in this stage of life. I pray
that they will be treated with the respect they deserve. I pray
that they will have life-giving relationships with family and
friends. Most of all, I pray that they will enjoy a life-giving
relationship with you and that they will place their hope in
Jesus, the resurrection and the life. Amen.

Romans 15:13
May the God of hope fill you with all joy and peace as you trust in him, so that you may overflow with hope by the power of the Holy Spirit. Amen.

FRIDAY
PRAYERS

WYOMING

NO
THRU
TRAFFIC

Friday Morning

John 4:23
Yet a time is coming and has now come when the true worshipers will worship the Father in the Spirit and in truth, for they are the kind of worshipers the Father seeks.

The Jesus Creed
Love the Lord your God with all your heart and with all your soul and with all your mind and with all your strength; and love your neighbor as yourself.

Confession of Sin
Let us confess our sins against God and our neighbor.

Silence may be kept.

Most merciful God,
I confess that I have sinned against you
in thought, word, and deed,
by what I have done,
and by what I have left undone.
I have not loved you with my whole heart;
I have not loved my neighbor as myself.
I am truly sorry and I humbly repent.
For the sake of your Son Jesus Christ,
have mercy on me and forgive me;
that I may delight in your will,
and walk in your ways,
to the glory of your Name. Amen.

Lord, open our lips. And our mouth shall proclaim your praise.

The Gloria
Glory to the Father, and to the Son, and to the Holy Spirit: as it was in the beginning, is now, and will be for ever. Amen.

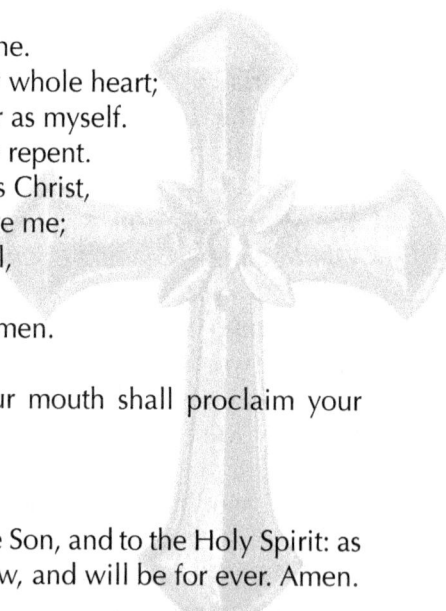

Worship the Lord in the beauty of holiness: Come let us adore him.

Psalter: Psalm 126
When the LORD restored the fortunes of Zion,
   we were like those who dreamed.
Our mouths were filled with laughter,
   our tongues with songs of joy.
Then it was said among the nations,
   "The LORD has done great things for them."
The LORD has done great things for us,
   and we are filled with joy.

Restore our fortunes, LORD,
   like streams in the Negev.
Those who sow with tears
   will reap with songs of joy.
Those who go out weeping,
   carrying seed to sow,
will return with songs of joy,
   carrying sheaves with them.

The Gloria
Glory to the Father, and to the Son, and to the Holy Spirit: as it was in the beginning, is now, and will be for ever. Amen.

The Morning Lesson
Old Testament Reading (found on pages 159 to 171)

The Morning Song—*A Song to the Lamb (Rev. 4:11 5:9-13)*
You are worthy, our Lord and God, to receive glory and honor and power, for you created all things, and by your will they were created and have their being.

You are worthy to take the scroll and to open its seals, because you were slain, and with your blood you purchased for God persons from every tribe and language and people and nation. You have made them to be a kingdom and priests to serve our God, and they will reign on the earth.

Worthy is the Lamb, who was slain, to receive power and wealth and wisdom and strength and honor and glory and praise!"

To him who sits on the throne and to the Lamb be praise and honor and glory and power, for ever and ever!

The Apostles' Creed
I believe in God, the Father almighty,
Creator of heaven and earth.

I believe in Jesus Christ, his only Son, our Lord.
He was conceived by the power of the Holy Spirit
and born of the Virgin Mary.
He suffered under Pontius Pilate,
was crucified, died, and was buried.
He descended to the dead.
On the third day he rose again.
He ascended into heaven,
and is seated at the right hand of the Father.
He will come again to judge the living and the dead.

I believe in the Holy Spirit,
the holy catholic Church,
the communion of saints,
the forgiveness of sins,
the resurrection of the body,
and the life everlasting. Amen.

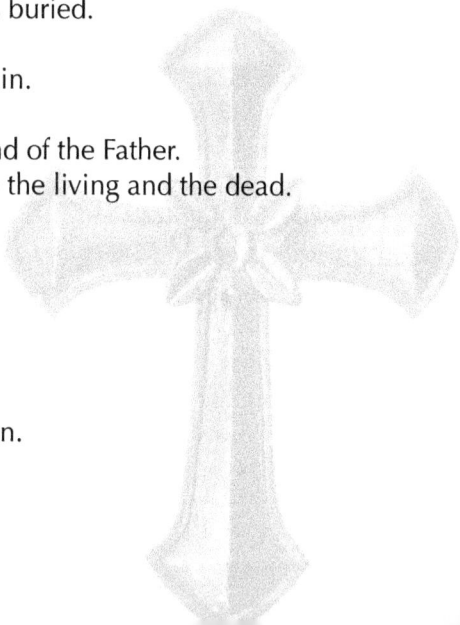

The Prayer of Our Lord

Our Father in heaven, hallowed be your Name,
your kingdom come, your will be done,
on earth as it is in heaven.
Give us today our daily bread.
Forgive us our sins as we forgive those who sin against us.
Lead us not into temptation, but deliver us from evil.
For the kingdom, the power, and the glory are yours,
now and for ever. Amen.

Prayer for the Day

Almighty God, whose most dear Son went not up to joy but
first he suffered pain, and entered not into glory before he
was crucified: Mercifully grant that we, walking in the way
of the cross, may find it none other than the way of life and
peace; through Jesus Christ your Son our Lord. Amen.

Prayer for My City (2 Corinthians 5:11-6:2)

Father, I praise you that you have reconciled the world to
yourself in Christ Jesus and have given us the ministry of
reconciliation. I pray for those in Wyoming who have not
yet responded in faith to your call of salvation and who are
therefore living apart from you. I pray that they will repent
and place their faith in Christ, who, though He knew no
sin, became sin for us, taking the punishment we deserved.
Forgive their sins and give them the righteousness of God.
Reconcile them to yourself. Make them a new creation. I
also pray that you will grant us the joy of participating with
you in the ministry of reconciliation. Amen.

2 Corinthians 13:14

May the grace of the Lord Jesus Christ, and the love of God,
and the fellowship of the Holy Spirit be with you all. Amen.

Friday Afternoon

O God, make speed to save us; Lord, make haste to help us.

The Gloria
Glory to the Father, and to the Son, and to the Holy Spirit: as it was in the beginning, is now, and will be for ever. Amen.

Hymn Selection—*Joyful, Joyful We Adore Thee*
Joyful, joyful, we adore Thee,
God of glory, Lord of love;
Hearts unfold like flow'rs before Thee,
Op'ning to the sun above.
Melt the clouds of sin and sadness;
Drive the dark of doubt away;
Giver of immortal gladness,
Fill us with the light of day!

All Thy works with joy surround Thee,
Earth and heav'n reflect Thy rays,
Stars and angels sing around Thee,
Center of unbroken praise.
Field and forest, vale and mountain,
Flow'ry meadow, flashing sea,
Singing bird and flowing fountain
Call us to rejoice in Thee.

Mortals, join the happy chorus,
Which the morning stars began;
Father love is reigning o'er us,
Brother love binds man to man.
Ever singing, march we onward,
Victors in the midst of strife,
Joyful music leads us Sunward
In the triumph song of life.

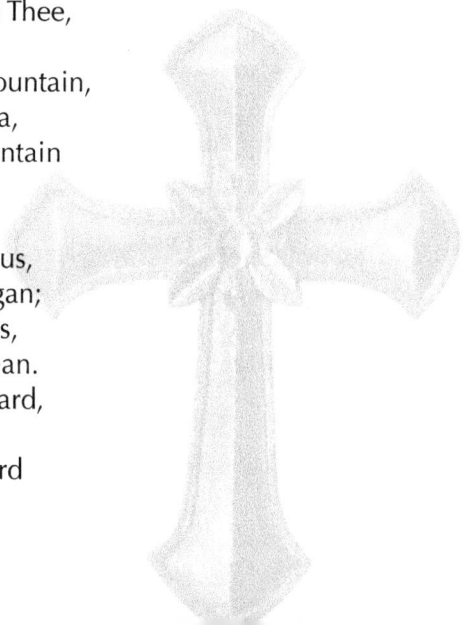

Psalm 130
Out of the depths I cry to you, LORD;
Lord, hear my voice.
Let your ears be attentive
  to my cry for mercy.

If you, LORD, kept a record of sins,
  Lord, who could stand?
But with you there is forgiveness,
  so that we can, with reverence, serve you.

I wait for the LORD, my whole being waits,
  and in his word I put my hope.
I wait for the Lord
  more than watchmen wait for the morning,
  more than watchmen wait for the morning.

Israel, put your hope in the LORD,
  for with the LORD is unfailing love
  and with him is full redemption.
He himself will redeem Israel
  from all their sins.

The Gloria
Glory to the Father, and to the Son, and to the Holy Spirit: as
it was in the beginning, is now, and will be for ever. Amen.

Jeremiah 29:11
For I know the plans I have for you," declares the LORD,
"plans to prosper you and not to harm you, plans to give
you hope and a future.

Silence
Lord, have mercy. Christ, have mercy. Lord, have mercy.

The Prayer of Our Lord

Our Father in heaven, hallowed be your Name,
your kingdom come, your will be done,
on earth as it is in heaven.
Give us today our daily bread.
Forgive us our sins as we forgive those who sin against us.
Lead us not into temptation, but deliver us from evil.
For the kingdom, the power, and the glory are yours,
now and for ever. Amen.

A few moments of intercessory prayer
Lord, hear our prayer; And let our cry come to you.

Holy Day Prayer *(found on pages 131 to 158)*

Prayer for My City

Father God, creator, sustainer, and provider, all good things
come from your hand. I pray that you will bless the city of
Wyoming with economic prosperity. I pray that new businesses and industries will invest in the area and that existing
businesses and industries will find success. I pray that those
seeking jobs will find gainful employment. I pray that those
in debt will find their way to financial stability. Finally Lord,
I pray that all in Wyoming will find sufficiency and contentment in you, and that, as you bless the city, those blessings
will be turned back to praise to you. Amen.

Prayer for the Afternoon

O God of all the nations of the earth: Remember the
multitudes who have been created in your image but have
not known the redeeming work of our Savior Jesus Christ;
and grant that, by the prayers and labors of your holy
Church, they may be brought to know and worship you as
you have been revealed in your Son; who lives and reigns
with you and the Holy Spirit, one God, for ever and ever.
Amen.

Friday Evening

Psalm 139:11-12
If I say, "Surely the darkness will hide me and the light become night around me," even the darkness will not be dark to you; the night will shine like the day, for darkness is as light to you.

The Jesus Creed
Love the Lord your God with all your heart and with all your soul and with all your mind and with all your strength; and love your neighbor as yourself.

Confession of Sin
Let us confess our sins against God and our neighbor.

Silence may be kept.

Most merciful God,
I confess that I have sinned against you
in thought, word, and deed,
by what I have done,
and by what I have left undone.
I have not loved you with my whole heart;
I have not loved my neighbor as myself.
I am truly sorry and I humbly repent.
For the sake of your Son Jesus Christ,
have mercy on me and forgive me;
that I may delight in your will,
and walk in your ways,
to the glory of your Name. Amen.

O God, make speed to save us; Lord, make haste to help us.

The Gloria
Glory to the Father, and to the Son, and to the Holy Spirit: as it was in the beginning, is now, and will be for ever. Amen.

O Gracious Light
O gracious Light,
pure brightness of the everliving Father in heaven,
O Jesus Christ, holy and blessed!

Now as we come to the setting of the sun,
and our eyes behold the vesper light,
we sing your praises, O God: Father, Son, and Holy Spirit.

You are worthy at all times to be praised by happy voices,
O Son of God, O Giver of life,
and to be glorified through all the worlds.

The Evening Psalter—*Psalm 15*
LORD, who may dwell in your sacred tent?
   Who may live on your holy mountain?

The one whose walk is blameless,
   who does what is righteous,
   who speaks the truth from their heart;
whose tongue utters no slander,
   who does no wrong to a neighbor,
   and casts no slur on others;
who despises a vile person
   but honors those who fear the LORD;
who keeps an oath even when it hurts,
   and does not change their mind;
who lends money to the poor without interest;
   who does not accept a bribe against the innocent.

Whoever does these things
   will never be shaken.

The Gloria
Glory to the Father, and to the Son, and to the Holy Spirit: as
it was in the beginning, is now, and will be for ever. Amen.

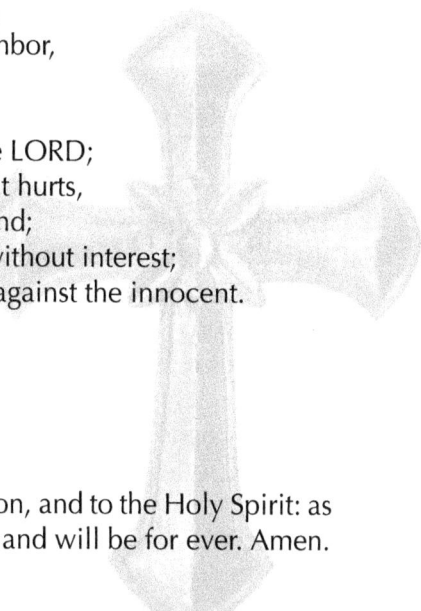

The Evening Lesson
New Testament Reading (found on pages 159 to 171)

The Apostles' Creed
I believe in God, the Father almighty,
Creator of heaven and earth.

I believe in Jesus Christ, his only Son, our Lord.
He was conceived by the power of the Holy Spirit
and born of the Virgin Mary.
He suffered under Pontius Pilate,
was crucified, died, and was buried.
He descended to the dead.
On the third day he rose again.
He ascended into heaven,
and is seated at the right hand of the Father.
He will come again to judge the living and the dead.

I believe in the Holy Spirit,
the holy catholic Church,
the communion of saints,
the forgiveness of sins,
the resurrection of the body,
and the life everlasting. Amen.

The Prayer of Our Lord
Our Father in heaven, hallowed be your Name,
your kingdom come, your will be done,
on earth as it is in heaven.
Give us today our daily bread.
Forgive us our sins as we forgive those who sin against us.
Lead us not into temptation, but deliver us from evil.
For the kingdom, the power, and the glory are yours,
now and for ever. Amen.

Prayer of Suffrage

Lord, we entreat you that this evening may be holy, good, and peaceful, that your holy angels may lead us in paths of peace and goodwill, that we may be pardoned and forgiven for our sins and offenses, that there may be peace to your Church and to the whole world, that we may depart this life in your faith and fear, and not be condemned before the great judgment seat of Christ, that we may be bound together by your Holy Spirit in the communion of all your saints, entrusting one another and all our life to Christ. To all of this we entreat you, Lord Christ. Amen.

Prayer for the Evening

Lord Jesus Christ, by your death you took away the sting of death: Grant to us your servants so to follow in faith where you have led the way, that we may at length fall asleep peacefully in you and wake up in your likeness; for your tender mercies' sake. Amen.

The General Thanksgiving

Almighty God, Father of all mercies,
we your unworthy servants give you humble thanks
for all your goodness and loving kindness
to us and to all whom you have made.

We bless you for our creation, preservation,
and all the blessings of this life;
but above all for your immeasurable love
in the redemption of the world by our Lord Jesus Christ;
for the means of grace, and for the hope of glory.

And, we pray, give us such an awareness of your mercies,
that with truly thankful hearts we may show forth your
praise, not only with our lips, but in our lives,
by giving up our selves to your service,
and by walking before you

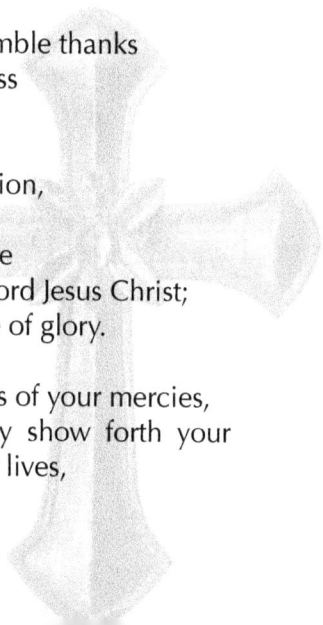

in holiness and righteousness all our days;
through Jesus Christ our Lord,
to whom, with you and the Holy Spirit,
be honor and glory throughout all ages. Amen.

Keep watch, dear Lord, with those who work, or watch, or weep this night, and give your angels charge over those who sleep. Tend the sick, Lord Christ; give rest to the weary, bless the dying, soothe the suffering, pity the afflicted, shield the joyous; and all for your love's sake. Amen.

Prayer for My City
Father, I pray for the handicapped in Wyoming. Please provide them with families, friends, and various institutions to help them lead vibrant and healthy lives. I pray for those struggling with discouragement, that they will find sufficiency and completeness in you. I pray for those dealing with a mental illness, that you will heal their minds and grant them peace. Father, I also pray for caregivers. Grant them energy, perseverance, and compassionate spirits. I pray that you will use those in the Church who are gifted with compassion to encourage and build up others, as agents of your grace. Amen.

Ephesians 3:20-21
Now to him who is able to do immeasurably more than all we ask or imagine, according to his power that is at work within us, to him be glory in the church and in Christ Jesus throughout all generations, for ever and ever! Amen.

SATURDAY
PRAYERS

Isaiah 57:15
For this is what the high and exalted One says— he who lives forever, whose name is holy: "I live in a high and holy place, but also with the one who is contrite and lowly in spirit, to revive the spirit of the lowly and to revive the heart of the contrite.

The Jesus Creed
Love the Lord your God with all your heart and with all your soul and with all your mind and with all your strength; and love your neighbor as yourself.

Confession of Sin
Let us confess our sins against God and our neighbor.

Silence may be kept.

Most merciful God,
I confess that I have sinned against you
in thought, word, and deed,
by what I have done,
and by what I have left undone.
I have not loved you with my whole heart;
I have not loved my neighbor as myself.
I am truly sorry and I humbly repent.
For the sake of your Son Jesus Christ,
have mercy on me and forgive me;
that I may delight in your will,
and walk in your ways,
to the glory of your Name. Amen.

Lord, open our lips. And our mouth shall proclaim your praise.

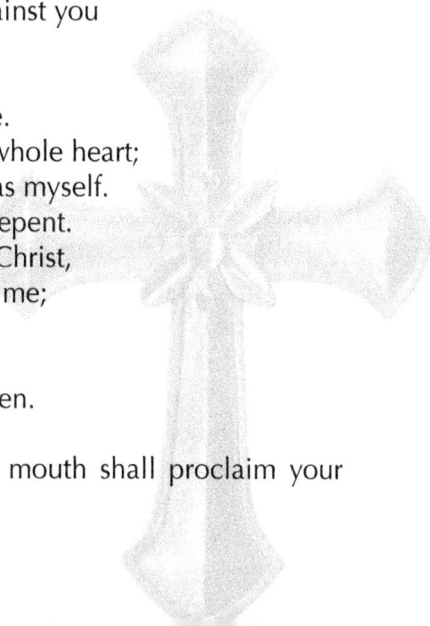

The Gloria
Glory to the Father, and to the Son, and to the Holy Spirit: as it was in the beginning, is now, and will be for ever. Amen.

Worship the Lord in the beauty of holiness: Come let us adore him.

Psalter: Psalm 91
Whoever dwells in the shelter of the Most High
　　will rest in the shadow of the Almighty.
I will say of the LORD, "He is my refuge and my fortress,
　　my God, in whom I trust."
Surely he will save you
　　from the fowler's snare
　　and from the deadly pestilence.
He will cover you with his feathers,
　　and under his wings you will find refuge;
　　his faithfulness will be your shield and rampart.
You will not fear the terror of night,
　　nor the arrow that flies by day,
nor the pestilence that stalks in the darkness,
　　nor the plague that destroys at midday.
A thousand may fall at your side,
　　ten thousand at your right hand,
　　but it will not come near you.
You will only observe with your eyes
　　and see the punishment of the wicked.

If you say, "The LORD is my refuge,"
　　and you make the Most High your dwelling,
no harm will overtake you,
　　no disaster will come near your tent.
For he will command his angels concerning you
　　to guard you in all your ways;
they will lift you up in their hands,
　　so that you will not strike your foot against a stone.

You will tread on the lion and the cobra;
  you will trample the great lion and the serpent.

"Because he loves me," says the LORD, "I will rescue him;
  I will protect him, for he acknowledges my name.
He will call on me, and I will answer him;
  I will be with him in trouble,
  I will deliver him and honor him.
With long life I will satisfy him
  and show him my salvation."

The Gloria
Glory to the Father, and to the Son, and to the Holy Spirit: as
it was in the beginning, is now, and will be for ever. Amen.

The Morning Lesson
Old Testament Reading (found on pages 159 to 171)

The Morning Song—*Glory to God*
Glory to God in the highest,
  and peace to his people on earth.
Lord God, heavenly King,
  almighty God and Father,
we worship you, we give you thanks,
  we praise you for your glory.
Lord Jesus Christ, only Son of the Father,
  Lord God, Lamb of God,
you take away the sin of the world;
  have mercy on us;
you are seated at the right hand of the Father;
  receive our prayer.
For you alone are the Holy One,
  you alone are the Lord,
you alone are the Most High, Jesus Christ,
  with the Holy Spirit,
  in the glory of God the Father. Amen.

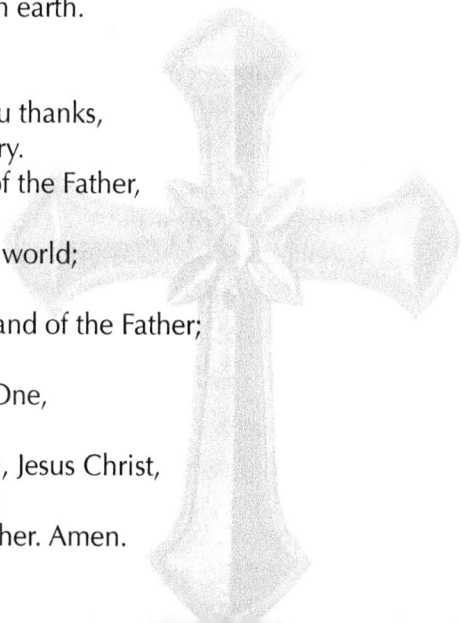

The Apostles' Creed

I believe in God, the Father almighty,
Creator of heaven and earth.

I believe in Jesus Christ, his only Son, our Lord.
He was conceived by the power of the Holy Spirit
and born of the Virgin Mary.
He suffered under Pontius Pilate,
was crucified, died, and was buried.
He descended to the dead.
On the third day he rose again.
He ascended into heaven,
and is seated at the right hand of the Father.
He will come again to judge the living and the dead.

I believe in the Holy Spirit,
the holy catholic Church,
the communion of saints,
the forgiveness of sins,
the resurrection of the body,
and the life everlasting. Amen.

The Prayer of Our Lord

Our Father in heaven, hallowed be your Name,
your kingdom come, your will be done,
on earth as it is in heaven.
Give us today our daily bread.
Forgive us our sins as we forgive those who sin against us.
Lead us not into temptation, but deliver us from evil.
For the kingdom, the power, and the glory are yours,
now and for ever. Amen.

Prayer for the Day

Almighty God, who after the creation of the world rested
from all you works and sanctified a day of rest for all your
creatures: Grant that we, putting away all earthly anxiet-

ies, may be duly prepared for the service of your sanctuary, and that our rest here upon earth may be a preparation for the eternal rest promised to your people in heaven; through Jesus Christ our Lord. Amen.

Prayer for My City (1 John 2:15-17)
Heavenly Father, teach the people of Wyoming to love you with all of their hearts, minds, souls, and strength, and to love their neighbors as themselves. Teach us to throw off all idols and false gods. Keep us from the sins of the lust of the eyes, the lust of the flesh, and the pride of life. We acknowledge that all those things pass away with the world and that if we love those things more than you, we will pass away with them. But we thank you that those who turn to you in faith will live forever. Turn our eyes, and the eyes of those in Wyoming, away from false gods to worship you alone. Amen.

Ephesians 3:20-21
Now to him who is able to do immeasurably more than all we ask or imagine, according to his power that is at work within us, to him be glory in the church and in Christ Jesus throughout all generations, for ever and ever! Amen.

Saturday Afternoon

O God, make speed to save us; Lord, make haste to help us.

The Gloria
Glory to the Father, and to the Son, and to the Holy Spirit: as it was in the beginning, is now, and will be for ever. Amen.

Hymn Selection—*Amazing Grace*
Amazing grace! How sweet the sound
That saved a wretch like me!
I once was lost, but now am found;
Was blind, but now I see.

'Twas grace that taught my heart to fear,
And grace my fears relieved;
How precious did that grace appear
The hour I first believed.

Through many dangers, toils and snares,
I have already come;
'Tis grace hath brought me safe thus far,
And grace will lead me home.

The Lord has promised good to me,
His Word my hope secures;
He will my Shield and Portion be,
As long as life endures.

When we've been there ten thousand years,
Bright shining as the sun,
We've no less days to sing God's praise
Than when we'd first begun.

Psalm 128
Blessed are all who fear the LORD,

who walk in obedience to him.
You will eat the fruit of your labor;
    blessings and prosperity will be yours.
Your wife will be like a fruitful vine
    within your house;
your children will be like olive shoots
    around your table.
Yes, this will be the blessing
    for the man who fears the LORD.

May the LORD bless you from Zion;
    may you see the prosperity of Jerusalem
    all the days of your life.
May you live to see your children's children—
    peace be on Israel.

The Gloria
Glory to the Father, and to the Son, and to the Holy Spirit: as it was in the beginning, is now, and will be for ever. Amen.

Hebrews 4:14-16
Therefore, since we have a great high priest who has ascended into heaven, Jesus the Son of God, let us hold firmly to the faith we profess. For we do not have a high priest who is unable to empathize with our weaknesses, but we have one who has been tempted in every way, just as we are—yet he did not sin. Let us then approach God's throne of grace with confidence, so that we may receive mercy and find grace to help us in our time of need.

Silence
Lord, have mercy. Christ, have mercy. Lord, have mercy.

The Prayer of Our Lord
Our Father in heaven, hallowed be your Name,
your kingdom come, your will be done,

on earth as it is in heaven.
Give us today our daily bread.
Forgive us our sins as we forgive those who sin against us.
Lead us not into temptation, but deliver us from evil.
For the kingdom, the power, and the glory are yours,
now and for ever. Amen.

A few moments of intercessory prayer
Lord, hear our prayer; And let our cry come to you.

Holy Day Prayer *(found on pages 131 to 158)*

Prayer for My City
Father God, you have appointed leaders in public office to
serve you as they serve the public. Please be with the city
leaders of Wyoming. Thank you for the wisdom you have
already shown them in the administration of the city. I pray
that you will give them knowledge and insight as they seek
to manage budgets, improve the financial stability of the
city, build and repair infrastructure, support public safety, and conduct all other matters of city administration. I
pray that you will protect the city from political scandal,
corruption, and damaging political divisiveness. I pray that
city leaders will promote the cause of justice and the common good as they serve you. Amen.

Prayer for the Afternoon
O God of all the nations of the earth: Remember the
multitudes who have been created in your image but have
not known the redeeming work of our Savior Jesus Christ;
and grant that, by the prayers and labors of your holy
Church, they may be brought to know and worship you as
you have been revealed in your Son; who lives and reigns
with you and the Holy Spirit, one God, for ever and ever.
Amen.

Saturday Evening

Amos 5:8
He who made the Pleiades and Orion, who turns midnight into dawn and darkens day into night, who calls for the waters of the sea and pours them out over the face of the land—the LORD is his name.

The Jesus Creed
Love the Lord your God with all your heart and with all your soul and with all your mind and with all your strength; and love your neighbor as yourself.

Confession of Sin
Let us confess our sins against God and our neighbor.

Silence may be kept.

Most merciful God,
I confess that I have sinned against you
in thought, word, and deed,
by what I have done,
and by what I have left undone.
I have not loved you with my whole heart;
I have not loved my neighbor as myself.
I am truly sorry and I humbly repent.
For the sake of your Son Jesus Christ,
have mercy on me and forgive me;
that I may delight in your will,
and walk in your ways,
to the glory of your Name. Amen.

O God, make speed to save us; Lord, make haste to help us.

The Gloria
Glory to the Father, and to the Son, and to the Holy Spirit: as it was in the beginning, is now, and will be for ever. Amen.

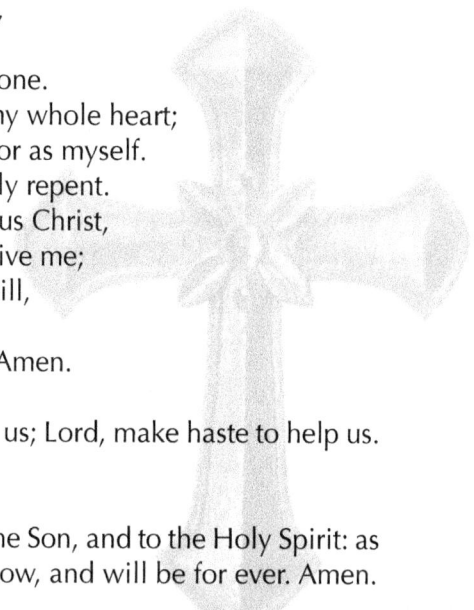

O Gracious Light
O gracious Light,
pure brightness of the everliving Father in heaven,
O Jesus Christ, holy and blessed!

Now as we come to the setting of the sun,
and our eyes behold the vesper light,
we sing your praises, O God: Father, Son, and Holy Spirit.

You are worthy at all times to be praised by happy voices,
O Son of God, O Giver of life,
and to be glorified through all the worlds.

The Evening Psalter—*Psalm 46*
God is our refuge and strength,
    an ever-present help in trouble.
Therefore we will not fear, though the earth give way
    and the mountains fall into the heart of the sea,
though its waters roar and foam
    and the mountains quake with their surging.

There is a river whose streams make glad the city of God,
    the holy place where the Most High dwells.
God is within her, she will not fall;
    God will help her at break of day.
Nations are in uproar, kingdoms fall;
    he lifts his voice, the earth melts.

The LORD Almighty is with us;
    the God of Jacob is our fortress.

Come and see what the LORD has done,
    the desolations he has brought on the earth.
He makes wars cease
    to the ends of the earth.
He breaks the bow and shatters the spear;

he burns the shields with fire.
He says, "Be still, and know that I am God;
  I will be exalted among the nations,
  I will be exalted in the earth."

The LORD Almighty is with us;
  the God of Jacob is our fortress.

The Gloria
Glory to the Father, and to the Son, and to the Holy Spirit: as it was in the beginning, is now, and will be for ever. Amen.

The Evening Lesson
New Testament Reading (found on pages 159 to 171)

The Apostles' Creed
I believe in God, the Father almighty,
Creator of heaven and earth.

I believe in Jesus Christ, his only Son, our Lord.
He was conceived by the power of the Holy Spirit
and born of the Virgin Mary.
He suffered under Pontius Pilate,
was crucified, died, and was buried.
He descended to the dead.
On the third day he rose again.
He ascended into heaven,
and is seated at the right hand of the Father.
He will come again to judge the living and the dead.

I believe in the Holy Spirit,
the holy catholic Church,
the communion of saints,
the forgiveness of sins,
the resurrection of the body,
and the life everlasting. Amen.

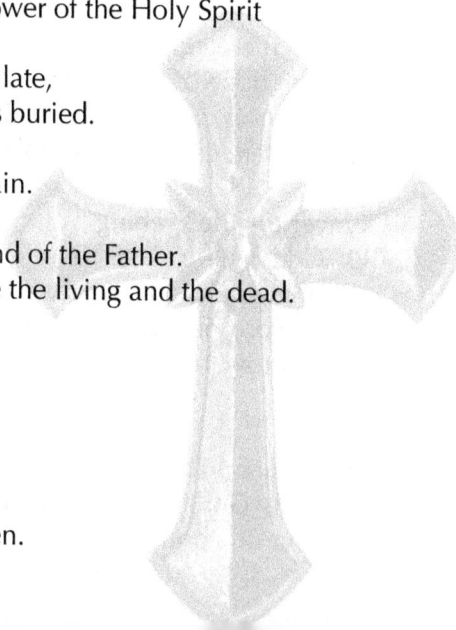

The Prayer of Our Lord
Our Father in heaven, hallowed be your Name,
your kingdom come, your will be done,
on earth as it is in heaven.
Give us today our daily bread.
Forgive us our sins as we forgive those who sin against us.
Lead us not into temptation, but deliver us from evil.
For the kingdom, the power, and the glory are yours,
now and for ever. Amen.

Prayer of Suffrage
Show us your mercy, O Lord;
And grant us your salvation.
Clothe your ministers with righteousness;
Let your people sing with joy.
Give peace, O Lord, in all the world;
For only in you can we live in safety.
Lord, keep this nation under your care;
And guide us in the way of justice and truth.
Let your way be known upon earth;
Your saving health among all nations.
Let not the needy, O Lord, be forgotten;
Nor the hope of the poor be taken away.
Create in us clean hearts, O God;
And sustain us with your Holy Spirit. Amen

Prayer for the Evening
O God, the source of eternal light: Shed forth your
unending day upon us who watch for you, that our lips may
praise you, our lives may bless you, and our worship on
the morrow give you glory; through Jesus Christ our Lord.
Amen.

The General Thanksgiving
Almighty God, Father of all mercies,
we your unworthy servants give you humble thanks

for all your goodness and loving kindness
to us and to all whom you have made.

We bless you for our creation, preservation,
and all the blessings of this life;
but above all for your immeasurable love
in the redemption of the world by our Lord Jesus Christ;
for the means of grace, and for the hope of glory.

And, we pray, give us such an awareness of your mercies,
that with truly thankful hearts we may show forth your
praise, not only with our lips, but in our lives,
by giving up our selves to your service,
and by walking before you
in holiness and righteousness all our days;
through Jesus Christ our Lord,
to whom, with you and the Holy Spirit,
be honor and glory throughout all ages. Amen.

O God, you manifest in your servants the signs of your
presence: Send forth upon us the Spirit of love, that in
companionship with one another your abounding grace
may increase among us; through Jesus Christ our Lord.
Amen.

Prayer for My City
Father God, you are right and just and fair. You show
no partiality. You defend the cause of the widow, the
orphan, and the foreigner against oppression. I pray for the
immigrants in Wyoming. I pray that they will not be
deprived of justice. I pray that the rule of law will be applied
equally to all. I pray that they will contribute to the health
of the community and be recognized for their contribution.
I pray that you will build bridges between the ethnic communities of Wyoming. I also pray that you will guide our

leaders to be wise, just, and fair, and I pray that they will craft immigration laws that are pleasing to you. Amen.

2 Corinthians 13:14
May the grace of the Lord Jesus Christ, and the love of God, and the fellowship of the Holy Spirit be with you all. Amen.

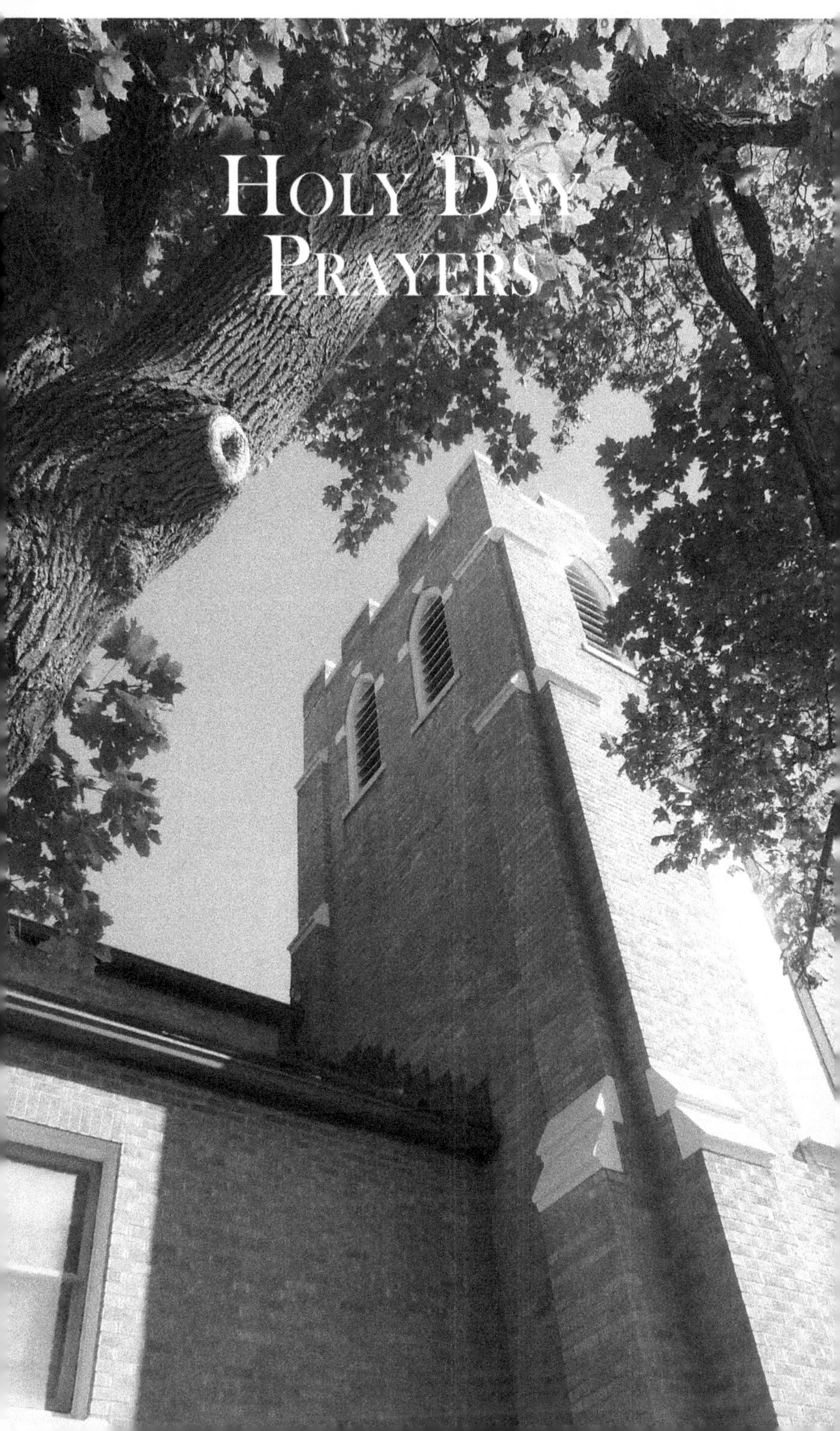

HOLY DAY
PRAYERS

Holy Days

January 18—Confession of Saint Peter
Almighty Father, who inspired Simon Peter, first among the apostles, to confess Jesus as Messiah and Son of the living God: Keep your Church steadfast upon the rock of this faith, so that in unity and peace we may proclaim the one truth and follow the one Lord, our Savior Jesus Christ; who lives and reigns with you and the Holy Spirit, one God, now and for ever. Amen.

January 25—Conversion of Saint Paul
O God, by the preaching of your apostle Paul you have caused the light of the Gospel to shine throughout the world: Grant, we pray, that we, having his wonderful conversion in remembrance, may show ourselves thankful to you by following his holy teaching; through Jesus Christ our Lord, who lives and reigns with you, in the unity of the Holy Spirit, one God, now and for ever. Amen.

February 2—The Presentation
Almighty and everliving God, we humbly pray that, as your only-begotten Son was this day presented in the temple, so we may be presented to you with pure and clean hearts by Jesus Christ our Lord; who lives and reigns with you and the Holy Spirit, one God, now and for ever. Amen.

February 24—Saint Matthias
Almighty God, who in the place of Judas chose your faithful servant Matthias to be numbered among the Twelve: Grant that your Church, being delivered from false apostles, may always be guided and governed by faithful and true pastors; through Jesus Christ our Lord, who lives and reigns with you, in the unity of the Holy Spirit, one God, now and for ever. Amen.

March 19—Saint Joseph

O God, who from the family of your servant David raised up Joseph to be the guardian of your incarnate Son and the spouse of his virgin mother: Give us grace to imitate his uprightness of life and his obedience to your commands; through Jesus Christ our Lord, who lives and reigns with you and the Holy Spirit, one God, for ever and ever. Amen.

March 25—The Annunciation

Pour your grace into our hearts, O Lord, that we who have known the incarnation of your Son Jesus Christ, announced by an angel to the Virgin Mary, may by his cross and passion be brought to the glory of his resurrection; who lives and reigns with you, in the unity of the Holy Spirit, one God, now and for ever. Amen.

April 25—Saint Mark

Almighty God, by the hand of Mark the evangelist you have given to your Church the Gospel of Jesus Christ the Son of God: We thank you for this witness, and pray that we may be firmly grounded in its truth; through Jesus Christ our Lord, who lives and reigns with you and the Holy Spirit, one God, for ever and ever. Amen.

May 1—Saint Philip and Saint James

Almighty God, who gave to your apostles Philip and James grace and strength to bear witness to the truth: Grant that we, being mindful of their victory of faith, may glorify in life and death the Name of our Lord Jesus Christ; who lives and reigns with you and the Holy Spirit, one God, now and for ever. Amen.

May 31—The Visitation

Father in heaven, by your grace the virgin mother of your i ncarnate Son was blessed in bearing him, but still more blessed in keeping your word: Grant us who honor the exaltation of her lowliness to follow the example of her devotion to your will; through Jesus Christ our Lord, who lives and reigns with you and the Holy Spirit, one God, for ever and ever. Amen.

June 11—Saint Barnabas
Grant, O God, that we may follow the example of your faithful servant Barnabas, who, seeking not his own renown but the well-being of your Church, gave generously of his life and substance for the relief of the poor and the spread of the Gospel; through Jesus Christ our Lord, who lives and reigns with you and the Holy Spirit, one God, for ever and ever. Amen.

June 24—The Nativity of Saint John the Baptist
Almighty God, by whose providence your servant John the Baptist was wonderfully born, and sent to prepare the way of your Son our Savior by preaching repentance: Make us so to follow his teaching and holy life, that we may truly repent according to his preaching; and, following his example, constantly speak the truth, boldly rebuke vice, and patiently suffer for the truth's sake; through Jesus Christ your Son our Lord, who lives and reigns with you and the Holy Spirit, one God, for ever and ever. Amen.

June 29—Saint Peter and Saint Paul
Almighty God, whose blessed apostles Peter and Paul glorified you by their martyrdom: Grant that your Church, instructed by their teaching and example, and knit together in unity by your Spirit, may ever stand firm upon the one foundation, which is Jesus Christ our Lord; who lives and reigns with you, in the unity of the Holy Spirit, one God, now and for ever. Amen.

July 4—Independence Day

Lord God Almighty, in whose Name the founders of this country won liberty for themselves and for us, and lit the torch of freedom for nations then unborn: Grant that we and all the people of this land may have grace to maintain our liberties in righteousness and peace; through Jesus Christ our Lord, who lives and reigns with you and the Holy Spirit, one God, for ever and ever. Amen.

July 22—Saint Mary Magdalene

Almighty God, whose blessed Son restored Mary Magdalene to health of body and of mind, and called her to be a witness of his resurrection: Mercifully grant that by your grace we may be healed from all our infirmities and know you in the power of his unending life; who with you and the Holy Spirit lives and reigns, one God, now and for ever. Amen.

July 25—Saint James

O gracious God, we remember before you today your servant and apostle James, first among the Twelve to suffer martyrdom for the Name of Jesus Christ; and we pray that you will pour out upon the leaders of your Church that spirit of self-denying service by which alone they may have true authority among your people; through Jesus Christ our Lord, who lives and reigns with you and the Holy Spirit, one God, now and for ever. Amen.

August 6—The Transfiguration

O God, who on the holy mount revealed to chosen witnesses your well-beloved Son, wonderfully transfigured, in raiment white and glistening: Mercifully grant that we, being delivered from the disquietude of this world, may by faith behold the King in his beauty; who with you, O Father, and you, O Holy Spirit, lives and reigns, one God, for ever and ever. Amen.

August 15—Saint Mary the Virgin

O God, you have taken to yourself the blessed Virgin Mary, mother of your incarnate Son: Grant that we, who have been redeemed by his blood, may share with her the glory of your eternal kingdom; through Jesus Christ our Lord, who lives and reigns with you, in the unity of the Holy Spirit, one God, now and for ever. Amen.

August 24—Saint Bartholomew

Almighty and everlasting God, who gave to your apostle Bartholomew grace truly to believe and to preach your Word: Grant that your Church may love what he believed and preach what he taught; through Jesus Christ our Lord, who lives and reigns with you and the Holy Spirit, one God, for ever and ever. Amen.

September 14—Holy Cross Day

Almighty God, whose Son our Savior Jesus Christ was lifted high upon the cross that he might draw the whole world to himself: Mercifully grant that we, who glory in the mystery of our redemption, may have grace to take up our cross and follow him; who lives and reigns with you and the Holy Spirit, one God, in glory everlasting. Amen.

September 21—Saint Matthew

We thank you, heavenly Father, for the witness of your apostle and evangelist Matthew to the Gospel of your Son our Savior; and we pray that, after his example, we may with ready wills and hearts obey the calling of our Lord to follow him; through Jesus Christ our Lord, who lives and reigns with you and the Holy Spirit, one God, now and for ever. Amen.

September 29— Saint Michael and All Angels

Everlasting God, you have ordained and constituted in a wonderful order the ministries of angels and mortals:

Mercifully grant that, as your holy angels always serve and worship you in heaven, so by your appointment they may help and defend us here on earth; through Jesus Christ our Lord, who lives and reigns with you and the Holy Spirit, one God, for ever and ever. Amen.

October 18—Saint Luke
Almighty God, who inspired your servant Luke the physician to set forth in the Gospel the love and healing power of your Son: Graciously continue in your Church this love and power to heal, to the praise and glory of your Name; through Jesus Christ our Lord, who lives and reigns with you, in the unity of the Holy Spirit, one God, now and for ever. Amen.

October 23—Saint James of Jerusalem
Grant, O God, that, following the example of your servant James the Just, brother of our Lord, your Church may give itself continually to prayer and to the reconciliation of all who are at variance and enmity; through Jesus Christ our Lord, who lives and reigns with you and the Holy Spirit, one God, now and for ever. Amen.

October 28—Saint Simon and Saint Jude
O God, we thank you for the glorious company of the apostles, and especially on this day for Simon and Jude; and we pray that, as they were faithful and zealous in their mission, so we may with ardent devotion make known the love and mercy of our Lord and Savior Jesus Christ; who lives and reigns with you and the Holy Spirit, one God, for ever and ever. Amen.

November 1—All Saints' Day
Almighty God, you have knit together your elect in one communion and fellowship in the mystical body of your Son Christ our Lord: Give us grace so to follow your blessed

saints in all virtuous and godly living, that we may come to those ineffable joys that you have prepared for those who truly love you; through Jesus Christ our Lord, who with you and the Holy Spirit lives and reigns, one God, in glory everlasting. Amen.

Thanksgiving Day

Almighty and gracious Father, we give you thanks for the fruits of the earth in their season and for the labors of those who harvest them. Make us, we pray, faithful stewards of your great bounty, for the provision of our necessities and the relief of all who are in need, to the glory of your Name; through Jesus Christ our Lord, who lives and reigns with you and the Holy Spirit, one God, now and for ever. Amen.

November 30—Saint Andrew

Almighty God, who gave such grace to your apostle Andrew that he readily obeyed the call of your Son Jesus Christ, and brought his brother with him: Give us, who are called by your holy Word, grace to follow him without delay, and to bring those near to us into his gracious presence; who lives and reigns with you and the Holy Spirit, one God, now and for ever. Amen.

December 21—Saint Thomas

Everliving God, who strengthened your apostle Thomas with firm and certain faith in your Son's resurrection: Grant us so perfectly and without doubt to believe in Jesus Christ, our Lord and our God, that our faith may never be found wanting in your sight; through him who lives and reigns with you and the Holy Spirit, one God, now and for ever. Amen.

December 26—Saint Stephen

We give you thanks, O Lord of glory, for the example of the first martyr Stephen, who looked up to heaven and prayed for his persecutors to your Son Jesus Christ, who stands at your right hand; where he lives and reigns with you and the Holy Spirit, one God, in glory everlasting. Amen.

December 27—Saint John
Shed upon your Church, O Lord, the brightness of your light, that we, being illumined by the teaching of your apostle and evangelist John, may so walk in the light of your truth, that at length we may attain to the fullness of eternal life; through Jesus Christ our Lord, who lives and reigns with you and the Holy Spirit, one God, for ever and ever. Amen.

December 28—The Holy Innocents
We remember today, O God, the slaughter of the holy innocents of Bethlehem by King Herod. Receive, we pray, into the arms of your mercy all innocent victims; and by your great might frustrate the designs of evil tyrants and establish your rule of justice, love, and peace; through Jesus Christ our Lord, who lives and reigns with you, in the unity of the Holy Spirit, one God, for ever and ever. Amen

January 1— The Holy Name
Eternal Father, you gave to your incarnate Son the holy name of Jesus to be the sign of our salvation: Plant in every heart, we pray, the love of him who is the Savior of the world, our Lord Jesus Christ; who lives and reigns with you and the Holy Spirit, one God, in glory everlasting. Amen.

Holy Seasons

THE SEASON OF EPIPHANY

January 6— The Epiphany
O God, by the leading of a star you manifested your only Son to the peoples of the earth: Lead us, who know you now by faith, to your presence, where we may see your glory face to face; through Jesus Christ our Lord, who lives and reigns with you and the Holy Spirit, one God, now and for ever. Amen.

First Sunday after the Epiphany: The Baptism of our Lord
Father in heaven, who at the baptism of Jesus in the River Jordan proclaimed him your beloved Son and anointed him with the Holy Spirit: Grant that all who are baptized into his Name may keep the covenant they have made, and boldly confess him as Lord and Savior; who with you and the Holy Spirit lives and reigns, one God, in glory everlasting. Amen.

Second Sunday after the Epiphany
Almighty God, whose Son our Savior Jesus Christ is the light of the world: Grant that your people, illumined by your Word and Sacraments, may shine with the radiance of Christ's glory, that he may be known, worshiped, and obeyed to the ends of the earth; through Jesus Christ our Lord, who with you and the Holy Spirit lives and reigns, one God, now and for ever. Amen.

Third Sunday after the Epiphany
Give us grace, O Lord, to answer readily the call of our Savior Jesus Christ and proclaim to all people the Good News of his salvation, that we and the whole world may perceive the glory of his marvelous works; who lives and reigns with you and the Holy Spirit, one God, for ever and ever. Amen.

Fourth Sunday after the Epiphany
Almighty and everlasting God, you govern all things both
in heaven and on earth: Mercifully hear the supplications of
your people, and in our time grant us your peace; through
Jesus Christ our Lord, who lives and reigns with you and the
Holy Spirit, one God, for ever and ever. Amen.

Fifth Sunday after the Epiphany
Set us free, O God, from the bondage of our sins, and give
us the liberty of that abundant life which you have made
known to us in your Son our Savior Jesus Christ; who lives
and reigns with you, in the unity of the Holy Spirit, one
God, now and for ever. Amen.

Sixth Sunday after the Epiphany
O God, the strength of all who put their trust in you:
Mercifully accept our prayers; and because in our weak-
ness we can do nothing good without you, give us the help
of your grace, that in keeping your commandments we may
please you both in will and deed; through Jesus Christ our
Lord, who lives and reigns with you and the Holy Spirit, one
God, for ever and ever. Amen.

Seventh Sunday after the Epiphany
O Lord, you have taught us that without love whatever we
do is worth nothing: Send your Holy Spirit and pour into
our hearts your greatest gift, which is love, the true bond
of peace and of all virtue, without which whoever lives is
accounted dead before you. Grant this for the sake of your
only Son Jesus Christ, who lives and reigns with you and the
Holy Spirit, one God, now and for ever. Amen.

Eighth Sunday after the Epiphany
Most loving Father, whose will it is for us to give thanks for
all things, to fear nothing but the loss of you, and to cast all
our care on you who care for us: Preserve us from faithless

fears and worldly anxieties, that no clouds of this mortal life may hide from us the light of that love which is immortal, and which you have manifested to us in your Son Jesus Christ our Lord; who lives and reigns with you, in the unity of the Holy Spirit, one God, now and for ever. Amen.

THE SEASON OF LENT

Ash Wednesday
Almighty and everlasting God, you hate nothing you have made and forgive the sins of all who are penitent: Create and make in us new and contrite hearts, that we, worthily lamenting our sins and acknowledging our wretchedness, may obtain of you, the God of all mercy, perfect remission and forgiveness; through Jesus Christ our Lord, who lives and reigns with you and the Holy Spirit, one God, for ever and ever. Amen.

First Sunday in Lent
Almighty God, whose blessed Son was led by the Spirit to be tempted by Satan: Come quickly to help us who are assaulted by many temptations; and, as you know the weaknesses of each of us, let each one find you mighty to save; through Jesus Christ your Son our Lord, who lives and reigns with you and the Holy Spirit, one God, now and for ever. Amen.

Second Sunday in Lent
O God, whose glory it is always to have mercy: Be gracious to all who have gone astray from your ways, and bring them again with penitent hearts and steadfast faith to embrace and hold fast the unchangeable truth of your Word, Jesus Christ your Son; who with you and the Holy Spirit lives and reigns, one God, for ever and ever. Amen.

Third Sunday in Lent

Almighty God, you know that we have no power in ourselves to help ourselves: Keep us both outwardly in our bodies and inwardly in our souls, that we may be defended from all adversities which may happen to the body, and from all evil thoughts which may assault and hurt the soul; through Jesus Christ our Lord, who lives and reigns with you and the Holy Spirit, one God, for ever and ever. Amen.

Fourth Sunday in Lent

Gracious Father, whose blessed Son Jesus Christ came down from heaven to be the true bread which gives life to the world: Evermore give us this bread, that he may live in us, and we in him; who lives and reigns with you and the Holy Spirit, one God, now and for ever. Amen.

Fifth Sunday in Lent

Almighty God, you alone can bring into order the unruly wills and affections of sinners: Grant your people grace to love what you command and desire what you promise; that, among the swift and varied changes of the world, our hearts may surely there be fixed where true joys are to be found; through Jesus Christ our Lord, who lives and reigns with you and the Holy Spirit, one God, now and for ever. Amen.

THE SEASON OF HOLY WEEK AND EASTER

Sunday of the Passion: Palm Sunday

Almighty and everliving God, in your tender love for the human race you sent your Son our Savior Jesus Christ to take upon him our nature, and to suffer death upon the cross, giving us the example of his great humility: Mercifully grant that we may walk in the way of his suffering, and also share in his resurrection; through Jesus Christ our Lord, who lives and reigns with you and the Holy Spirit, one God, for ever and ever. Amen.

Monday in Holy Week

Almighty God, whose most dear Son went not up to joy but first he suffered pain, and entered not into glory before he was crucified: Mercifully grant that we, walking in the way of the cross, may find it none other than the way of life and peace; through Jesus Christ your Son our Lord, who lives and reigns with you and the Holy Spirit, one God, for ever and ever. Amen.

Tuesday in Holy Week

O God, by the passion of your blessed Son you made an instrument of shameful death to be for us the means of life: Grant us so to glory in the cross of Christ, that we may gladly suffer shame and loss for the sake of your Son our Savior Jesus Christ; who lives and reigns with you and the Holy Spirit, one God, for ever and ever. Amen.

Wednesday in Holy Week

Lord God, whose blessed Son our Savior gave his body to be whipped and his face to be spit upon: Give us grace to accept joyfully the sufferings of the present time, confident of the glory that shall be revealed; through Jesus Christ your Son our Lord, who lives and reigns with you and the Holy Spirit, one God, for ever and ever. Amen.

Maundy Thursday

Almighty Father, whose dear Son, on the night before he suffered, instituted the Sacrament of his Body and Blood: Mercifully grant that we may receive it thankfully in remembrance of Jesus Christ our Lord, who in these holy mysteries gives us a pledge of eternal life; and who now lives and reigns with you and the Holy Spirit, one God, for ever and ever. Amen.

Good Friday

Almighty God, we pray you graciously to behold this your family, for whom our Lord Jesus Christ was willing to be betrayed, and given into the hands of sinners, and to suffer death upon the cross; who now lives and reigns with you and the Holy Spirit, one God, for ever and ever. Amen.

Holy Saturday

O God, Creator of heaven and earth: Grant that, as the crucified body of your dear Son was laid in the tomb and rested on this holy Sabbath, so we may await with him the coming of the third day, and rise with him to newness of life; who now lives and reigns with you and the Holy Spirit, one God, for ever and ever. Amen.

Easter Day

Almighty God, who through your only-begotten Son Jesus Christ overcame death and opened to us the gate of everlasting life: Grant that we, who celebrate with joy the day of the Lord's resurrection, may be raised from the death of sin by your life-giving Spirit; through Jesus Christ our Lord, who lives and reigns with you and the Holy Spirit, one God, now and for ever. Amen.

Monday in Easter Week

Grant, we pray, Almighty God, that we who celebrate with awe the Paschal feast may be found worthy to attain to everlasting joys; through Jesus Christ our Lord, who lives and reigns with you and the Holy Spirit, one God, now and for ever. Amen.

Tuesday in Easter Week

O God, who by the glorious resurrection of your Son Jesus Christ destroyed death and brought life and immortality to light: Grant that we, who have been raised with him, may abide in his presence and rejoice in the hope of eternal glory; through Jesus Christ our Lord, to whom, with you and the Holy Spirit, be dominion and praise for ever and ever. Amen.

Wednesday in Easter Week

O God, whose blessed Son made himself known to his disciples in the breaking of bread: Open the eyes of our faith, that we may behold him in all his redeeming work; who lives and reigns with you, in the unity of the Holy Spirit, one God, now and for ever. Amen.

Thursday in Easter Week

Almighty and everlasting God, who in the Paschal mystery established the new covenant of reconciliation: Grant that all who have been reborn into the fellowship of Christ's Body may show forth in their lives what they profess by their faith; through Jesus Christ our Lord, who lives and reigns with you and the Holy Spirit, one God, for ever and ever. Amen.

Friday in Easter Week

Almighty Father, who gave your only Son to die for our sins and to rise for our justification: Give us grace so to put away the leaven of malice and wickedness, that we may always serve you in pureness of living and truth; through Jesus Christ your Son our Lord, who lives and reigns with you and the Holy Spirit, one God, now and for ever. Amen.

Saturday in Easter Week

We thank you, heavenly Father, that you have delivered us from the dominion of sin and death and brought us into the kingdom of your Son; and we pray that, as by his death he has recalled us to life, so by his love he may raise us to eternal joys; who lives and reigns with you, in the unity of the Holy Spirit, one God, now and for ever. Amen.

Second Sunday of Easter
Almighty and everlasting God, who in the Paschal mystery
established the new covenant of reconciliation: Grant that
all who have been reborn into the fellowship of Christ's
Body may show forth in their lives what they profess by their
faith; through Jesus Christ our Lord, who lives and reigns
with you and the Holy Spirit, one God, for ever and ever.
Amen.

Third Sunday of Easter
O God, whose blessed Son made himself known to his
disciples in the breaking of bread: Open the eyes of our
faith, that we may behold him in all his redeeming work;
who lives and reigns with you, in the unity of the Holy
Spirit, one God, now and for ever. Amen.

Fourth Sunday of Easter
O God, whose Son Jesus is the good shepherd of your
people: Grant that when we hear his voice we may know
him who calls us each by name, and follow where he leads;
who, with you and the Holy Spirit, lives and reigns, one
God, for ever and ever. Amen.

Fifth Sunday of Easter
Almighty God, whom truly to know is everlasting life: Grant
us so perfectly to know your Son Jesus Christ to be the way,
the truth, and the life, that we may steadfastly follow his
steps in the way that leads to eternal life; through Jesus
Christ your Son our Lord, who lives and reigns with you,
in the unity of the Holy Spirit, one God, for ever and ever.
Amen.

Sixth Sunday of Easter
O God, you have prepared for those who love you such good
things as surpass our understanding: Pour into our hearts
such love towards you, that we, loving you in all things and

above all things, may obtain your promises, which exceed all that we can desire; through Jesus Christ our Lord, who lives and reigns with you and the Holy Spirit, one God, for ever and ever. Amen.

Ascension Day
Almighty God, whose blessed Son our Savior Jesus Christ ascended far above all heavens that he might fill all things: Mercifully give us faith to perceive that, according to his promise, he abides with his Church on earth, even to the end of the ages; through Jesus Christ our Lord, who lives and reigns with you and the Holy Spirit, one God, in glory everlasting. Amen.

Seventh Sunday of Easter: The Sunday after Ascension Day
O God, the King of glory, you have exalted your only Son Jesus Christ with great triumph to your kingdom in heaven: Do not leave us comfortless, but send us your Holy Spirit to strengthen us, and exalt us to that place where our Savior Christ has gone before; who lives and reigns with you and the Holy Spirit, one God, in glory everlasting. Amen.

The Season of Pentecost

The Day of Pentecost: Whitsunday
Almighty God, on this day you opened the way of eternal life to every race and nation by the promised gift of your Holy Spirit: Shed abroad this gift throughout the world by the preaching of the Gospel, that it may reach to the ends of the earth; through Jesus Christ our Lord, who lives and reigns with you, in the unity of the Holy Spirit, one God, for ever and ever. Amen.

First Sunday after Pentecost: Trinity Sunday
Almighty and everlasting God, you have given to us your servants grace, by the confession of a true faith, to acknowl-

edge the glory of the eternal Trinity, and in the power of your divine Majesty to worship the Unity: Keep us steadfast in this faith and worship, and bring us at last to see you in your one and eternal glory, O Father; who with the Son and the Holy Spirit live and reign, one God, for ever and ever. Amen.

Proper 1 *The Sunday closest to May 11*
Remember, O Lord, what you have wrought in us and not what we deserve; and, as you have called us to your service, make us worthy of our calling; through Jesus Christ our Lord, who lives and reigns with you and the Holy Spirit, one God, now and for ever. Amen.

Proper 2 *The Sunday closest to May 18*
Almighty and merciful God, in your goodness keep us, we pray, from all things that may hurt us, that we, being ready both in mind and body, may accomplish with free hearts those things which belong to your purpose; through Jesus Christ our Lord, who lives and reigns with you and the Holy Spirit, one God, now and for ever. Amen.

Proper 3 *The Sunday closest to May 25*
Grant, O Lord, that the course of this world may be peaceably governed by your providence; and that your Church may joyfully serve you in confidence and serenity; through Jesus Christ our Lord, who lives and reigns with you and the Holy Spirit, one God, for ever and ever. Amen.

Proper 4 *The Sunday closest to June 1*
O God, your never-failing providence sets in order all things both in heaven and earth: Put away from us, we entreat you, all hurtful things, and give us those things which are profitable for us; through Jesus Christ our Lord, who lives and reigns with you and the Holy Spirit, one God, for ever and ever. Amen.

Proper 5 *The Sunday closest to June 8*
O God, from whom all good proceeds: Grant that by your inspiration we may think those things that are right, and by your merciful guiding may do them; through Jesus Christ our Lord, who lives and reigns with you and the Holy Spirit, one God, for ever and ever. Amen.

Proper 6 *The Sunday closest to June 15*
Keep, O Lord, your household the Church in your steadfast faith and love, that through your grace we may proclaim your truth with boldness, and minister your justice with compassion; for the sake of our Savior Jesus Christ, who lives and reigns with you and the Holy Spirit, one God, now and for ever. Amen.

Proper 7 *The Sunday closest to June 22*
O Lord, make us have perpetual love and reverence for your holy Name, for you never fail to help and govern those whom you have set upon the sure foundation of your loving-kindness; through Jesus Christ our Lord, who lives and reigns with you and the Holy Spirit, one God, for ever and ever. Amen.

Proper 8 *The Sunday closest to June 29*
Almighty God, you have built your Church upon the foundation of the apostles and prophets, Jesus Christ himself being the chief cornerstone: Grant us so to be joined together in unity of spirit by their teaching, that we may be made a holy temple acceptable to you; through Jesus Christ our Lord, who lives and reigns with you and the Holy Spirit, one God, for ever and ever. Amen.

Proper 9 *The Sunday closest to July 6*
O God, you have taught us to keep all your commandments by loving you and our neighbor: Grant us the grace of your Holy Spirit, that we may be devoted to you with our

whole heart, and united to one another with pure affection; through Jesus Christ our Lord, who lives and reigns with you and the Holy Spirit, one God, for ever and ever. Amen.

Proper 10 *The Sunday closest to July 13*
O Lord, mercifully receive the prayers of your people who call upon you, and grant that they may know and understand what things they ought to do, and also may have grace and power faithfully to accomplish them; through Jesus Christ our Lord, who lives and reigns with you and the Holy Spirit, one God, now and for ever. Amen.

Proper 11 *The Sunday closest to July 20*
Almighty God, the fountain of all wisdom, you know our necessities before we ask and our ignorance in asking: Have compassion on our weakness, and mercifully give us those things which for our unworthiness we dare not, and for our blindness we cannot ask; through the worthiness of your Son Jesus Christ our Lord, who lives and reigns with you and the Holy Spirit, one God, now and for ever. Amen.

Proper 12 *The Sunday closest to July 27*
O God, the protector of all who trust in you, without whom nothing is strong, nothing is holy: Increase and multiply upon us your mercy; that, with you as our ruler and guide, we may so pass through things temporal, that we lose not the things eternal; through Jesus Christ our Lord, who lives and reigns with you and the Holy Spirit, one God, for ever and ever. Amen.

Proper 13 *The Sunday closest to August 3*
Let your continual mercy, O Lord, cleanse and defend your Church; and, because it cannot continue in safety without your help, protect and govern it always by your goodness; through Jesus Christ our Lord, who lives and reigns with you and the Holy Spirit, one God, for ever and ever. Amen.

Proper 14 *The Sunday closest to August 10*
Grant to us, Lord, we pray, the spirit to think and do always those things that are right, that we, who cannot exist without you, may by you be enabled to live according to your will; through Jesus Christ our Lord, who lives and reigns with you and the Holy Spirit, one God, for ever and ever. Amen.

Proper 15 *The Sunday closest to August 17*
Almighty God, you have given your only Son to be for us a sacrifice for sin, and also an example of godly life: Give us grace to receive thankfully the fruits of his redeeming work, and to follow daily in the blessed steps of his most holy life; through Jesus Christ your Son our Lord, who lives and reigns with you and the Holy Spirit, one God, now and for ever. Amen.

Proper 16 *The Sunday closest to August 24*
Grant, O merciful God, that your Church, being gathered together in unity by your Holy Spirit, may show forth your power among all peoples, to the glory of your Name; through Jesus Christ our Lord, who lives and reigns with you and the Holy Spirit, one God, for ever and ever. Amen.

Proper 17 *The Sunday closest to August 31*
Lord of all power and might, the author and giver of all good things: Graft in our hearts the love of your Name; increase in us true religion; nourish us with all goodness; and bring forth in us the fruit of good works; through Jesus Christ our Lord, who lives and reigns with you and the Holy Spirit, one God for ever and ever. Amen.

Proper 18 *The Sunday closest to September 7*
Grant us, O Lord, to trust in you with all our hearts; for, as you always resist the proud who confide in their own

strength, so you never forsake those who make their boast
of your mercy; through Jesus Christ our Lord, who lives and
reigns with you and the Holy Spirit, one God, now and for
ever. Amen.

Proper 19 *The Sunday closest to September 14*
O God, because without you we are not able to please you,
mercifully grant that your Holy Spirit may in all things direct
and rule our hearts; through Jesus Christ our Lord, who lives
and reigns with you and the Holy Spirit, one God, now and
for ever. Amen.

Proper 20 *The Sunday closest to September 21*
Grant us, Lord, not to be anxious about earthly things, but
to love things heavenly; and even now, while we are placed
among things that are passing away, to hold fast to those
that shall endure; through Jesus Christ our Lord, who lives
and reigns with you and the Holy Spirit, one God, for ever
and ever. Amen.

Proper 21 *The Sunday closest to September 28*
O God, you declare your almighty power chiefly in
showing mercy and pity: Grant us the fullness of your grace,
that we, running to obtain your promises, may become
partakers of your heavenly treasure; through Jesus Christ our
Lord, who lives and reigns with you and the Holy Spirit, one
God, for ever and ever. Amen.

Proper 22 *The Sunday closest to October 5*
Almighty and everlasting God, you are always more ready
to hear than we to pray, and to give more than we either
desire or deserve: Pour upon us the abundance of your
mercy, forgiving us those things of which our conscience is
afraid, and giving us those good things for which we are not
worthy to ask, except through the merits and mediation of
Jesus Christ our Savior; who lives and reigns with you and

the Holy Spirit, one God, for ever and ever. Amen.

Proper 23 *The Sunday closest to October 12*
Lord, we pray that your grace may always precede and follow us, that we may continually be given to good works; through Jesus Christ our Lord, who lives and reigns with you and the Holy Spirit, one God, now and for ever. Amen.

Proper 24 *The Sunday closest to October 19*
Almighty and everlasting God, in Christ you have revealed your glory among the nations: Preserve the works of your mercy, that your Church throughout the world may persevere with steadfast faith in the confession of your Name; through Jesus Christ our Lord, who lives and reigns with you and the Holy Spirit, one God, for ever and ever. Amen.

Proper 25 *The Sunday closest to October 26*
Almighty and everlasting God, increase in us the gifts of faith, hope, and charity; and, that we may obtain what you promise, make us love what you command; through Jesus Christ our Lord, who lives and reigns with you and the Holy Spirit, one God, for ever and ever. Amen.

Proper 26 *The Sunday closest to November 2*
Almighty and merciful God, it is only by your gift that your faithful people offer you true and laudable service: Grant that we may run without stumbling to obtain your heavenly promises; through Jesus Christ our Lord, who lives and reigns with you and the Holy Spirit, one God, now and for ever. Amen.

Proper 27 *The Sunday closest to November 9*
O God, whose blessed Son came into the world that he might destroy the works of the devil and make us children of God and heirs of eternal life: Grant that, having this hope,

we may purify ourselves as he is pure; that, when he comes again with power and great glory, we may be made like him in his eternal and glorious kingdom; where he lives and reigns with you and the Holy Spirit, one God, for ever and ever. Amen.

Proper 28 *The Sunday closest to November 16*
Blessed Lord, who caused all holy Scriptures to be written for our learning: Grant us so to hear them, read, mark, learn, and inwardly digest them, that we may embrace and ever hold fast the blessed hope of everlasting life, which you have given us in our Savior Jesus Christ; who lives and reigns with you and the Holy Spirit, one God, for ever and ever. Amen.

Proper 29 *The Sunday closest to November 23*
Almighty and everlasting God, whose will it is to restore all things in your well-beloved Son, the King of kings and Lord of lords: Mercifully grant that the peoples of the earth, divided and enslaved by sin, may be freed and brought together under his most gracious rule; who lives and reigns with you and the Holy Spirit, one God, now and for ever. Amen.

THE SEASON OF ADVENT

First Sunday of Advent
Almighty God, give us grace to cast away the works of darkness, and put on the armor of light, now in the time of this mortal life in which your Son Jesus Christ came to visit us in great humility; that in the last day, when he shall come again in his glorious majesty to judge both the living and the dead, we may rise to the life immortal; through him who lives and reigns with you and the Holy Spirit, one God, now and for ever. Amen.

Second Sunday of Advent

Merciful God, who sent your messengers the prophets to preach repentance and prepare the way for our salvation: Give us grace to heed their warnings and forsake our sins, that we may greet with joy the coming of Jesus Christ our Redeemer; who lives and reigns with you and the Holy Spirit, one God, now and for ever. Amen.

Third Sunday of Advent

Stir up your power, O Lord, and with great might come among us; and, because we are sorely hindered by our sins, let your bountiful grace and mercy speedily help and deliver us; through Jesus Christ our Lord, to whom, with you and the Holy Spirit, be honor and glory, now and for ever. Amen.

Fourth Sunday of Advent

Purify our conscience, Almighty God, by your daily visitation, that your Son Jesus Christ, at his coming, may find in us a mansion prepared for himself; who lives and reigns with you, in the unity of the Holy Spirit, one God, now and for ever. Amen.

The Nativity of Our Lord: Christmas Day, December 25

Almighty God, you have given your only-begotten Son to take our nature upon him, and to be born this day of a pure virgin: Grant that we, who have been born again and made your children by adoption and grace, may daily be renewed by your Holy Spirit; through our Lord Jesus Christ, to whom with you and the same Spirit be honor and glory, now and for ever. Amen.

First Sunday after Christmas Day

Almighty God, you have poured upon us the new light of your incarnate Word: Grant that this light, enkindled in our hearts, may shine forth in our lives; through Jesus Christ our

Lord, who lives and reigns with you, in the unity of the Holy Spirit, one God, now and for ever. Amen.

Second Sunday after Christmas Day

O God, who wonderfully created, and yet more wonderfully restored, the dignity of human nature: Grant that we may share the divine life of him who humbled himself to share our humanity, your Son Jesus Christ; who lives and reigns with you, in the unity of the Holy Spirit, one God, for ever and ever. Amen.

SCRIPTURE
READING PLANS

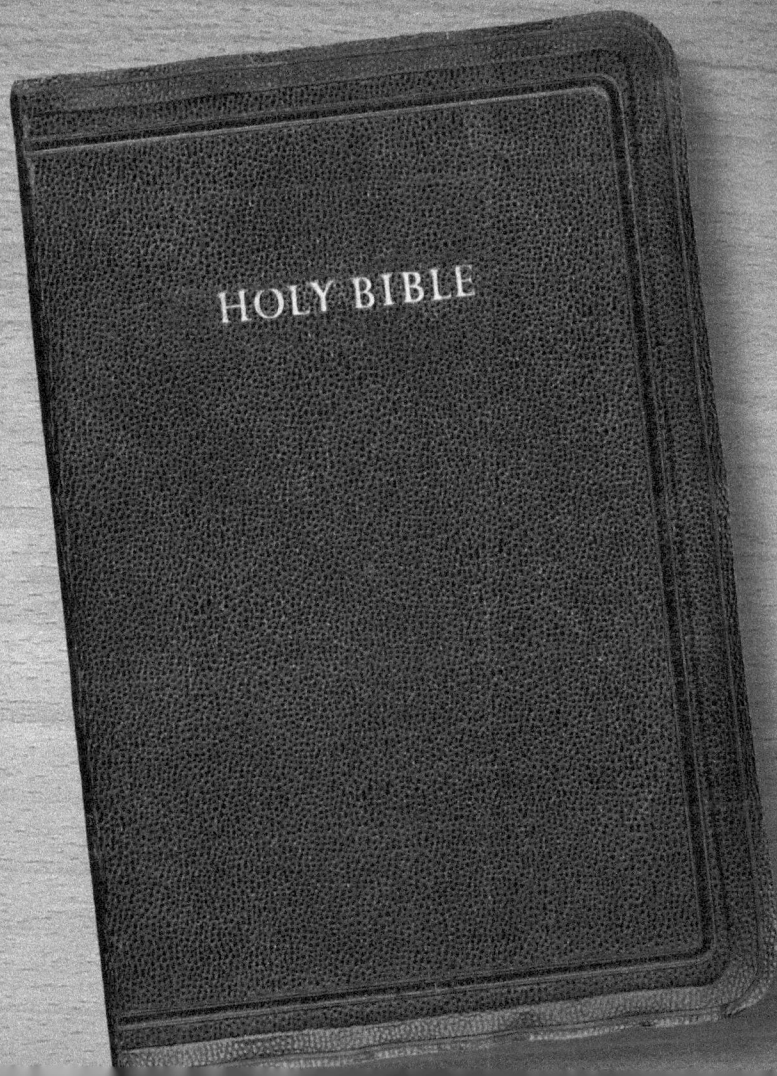

365 Day Reading Plan

This reading plan is designed for optimum flexibility by allowing for misses in reading, making reading through the Bible more manageable. It will still help you read through the Holy Scriptures from beginning to end, just at your own pace, whether through a year or not.

☐ Day 1: Gen 1-3; Matt 1
☐ Day 2: Gen 4-6; Matt 2
☐ Day 3: Gen 7-9; Matt 3
☐ Day 4: Gen 10-12; Matt 4
☐ Day 5: Gen 13-15; Matt 5:1-26
☐ Day 6: Gen 16-17; Matt 5:27-48
☐ Day 7: Gen 18-19; Matt 6:1-18
☐ Day 8: Gen 20-22; Matt 6:19-34
☐ Day 9: Gen 23-24; Matt 7
☐ Day 10: Gen 25-26; Matt 8:1-17
☐ Day 11: Gen 27-28; Matt 8:18-34
☐ Day 12: Gen 29-30; Matt 9:1-17
☐ Day 13: Gen 31-32; Matt 9:18-38
☐ Day 14: Gen 33-35; Matt 10:1-20
☐ Day 15: Gen 36-38; Matt 10:21-42
☐ Day 16: Gen 39-40; Matt 11
☐ Day 17: Gen 41-42; Matt 12:1-23
☐ Day 18: Gen 43-45; Matt 12:24-50
☐ Day 19: Gen 46-48; Matt 13:1-30
☐ Day 20: Gen 49-50; Matt 13:31-58
☐ Day 21: Ex 1-3; Matt 14:1-21
☐ Day 22: Ex 4-6; Matt 14:22-36
☐ Day 23: Ex 7-8; Matt 15:1-20
☐ Day 24: Ex 9-11; Matt 15:21-39
☐ Day 25: Ex 12-13; Matt 16
☐ Day 26: Ex 14-15; Matt 17
☐ Day 27: Ex 16-18; Matt 18:1-20
☐ Day 28: Ex 19-20; Matt 18:21-35
☐ Day 29: Ex 21-22; Matt 19
☐ Day 30: Ex 23-24; Matt 20:1-16
☐ Day 31: Ex 25-26; Matt 20:17-34

☐ Day 32: Ex 27-28; Matt 21:1-22
☐ Day 33: Ex 29-30; Matt 21:23-46
☐ Day 34: Ex 31-33; Matt 22: 1-22
☐ Day 35: Ex 34-35; Matt 22:23-46
☐ Day 36: Ex 36-38; Matt 23:1-22
☐ Day 37: Ex 39-40; Matt 23:23-39
☐ Day 38: Lev 1-3; Matt 24:1-28
☐ Day 39: Lev 4-5; Matt 24:29-51
☐ Day 40: Lev 6-7; Matt 25:1-30
☐ Day 41: Lev 8-10; Matt 25:31-46
☐ Day 42: Lev 11-12; Matt 26:1-25
☐ Day 43: Lev 13; Matt 26:26-50
☐ Day 44: Lev 14; Matt 26:51-75
☐ Day 45: Lev 15-16; Matt 27:1-26
☐ Day 46: Lev 17-18; Matt 27:27-50
☐ Day 47: Lev 19-20; Matt 27:51-66
☐ Day 48: Lev 21-22; Matt 28
☐ Day 49: Lev 23-24; Mark 1:1-22
☐ Day 50: Lev 25; Mark 1:23-45
☐ Day 51: Lev 26-27; Mark 2
☐ Day 52: Num 1-2; Mark 3:1-19
☐ Day 53: Num 3-4; Mark 3:20-35
☐ Day 54: Num 5-6; Mark 4:1-20
☐ Day 55: Num 7-8; Mark 4:21-41
☐ Day 56: Num 9-11; Mark 5:1-20
☐ Day 57: Num 12-14; Mark 5:21-43
☐ Day 58: Num 15-16; Mark 6:1-29
☐ Day 59: Num 17-19; Mark 6:30-56
☐ Day 60: Num 20-22; Mark 7:1-13
☐ Day 61: Num 23-25; Mark 7:14-37
☐ Day 62: Num 26-28; Mark 8

PRAYERS FOR MY CITY

- ☐ Day 63: Num 29-31; Mark 9:1-29
- ☐ Day 64: Num 32-34; Mark 9:30-50
- ☐ Day 65: Num 35-36; Mark 10:1-31
- ☐ Day 66: Deut 1-3; Mark 10:32-52
- ☐ Day 67: Deut 4-6; Mark 11:1-18
- ☐ Day 68: Deut 7-9; Mark 11:19-33
- ☐ Day 59: Deut 10-12; Mark 12:1-27
- ☐ Day 70: Deut 13-15; Mark 12:28-44
- ☐ Day 71: Deut 16-18; Mark 13:1-20
- ☐ Day 72: Deut 19-21; Mark 13:21-37
- ☐ Day 73: Deut 22-24; Mark 14:1-26
- ☐ Day 74: Deut 25-27; Mark 14:27-53
- ☐ Day 75: Deut 28-29; Mark 14:54-72
- ☐ Day 76: Deut 30-31; Mark 15:1-25
- ☐ Day 77: Deut 32-34; Mark 15:26-47
- ☐ Day 78: Josh 1-3; Mark 16
- ☐ Day 79: Josh 4-6; Luke 1:1-20
- ☐ Day 80: Josh 7-9; Luke 1:21-38
- ☐ Day 81: Josh 10-12; Luke 1:39-56
- ☐ Day 82: Josh 13-15; Luke 1:57-80
- ☐ Day 83: Josh 16-18; Luke 2:1-24
- ☐ Day 84: Josh 19-21; Luke 2:25-52
- ☐ Day 85: Josh 22-24; Luke 3
- ☐ Day 86: Jud 1-3; Luke 4:1-30
- ☐ Day 87: Jud 4-6; Luke 4:31-44
- ☐ Day 88: Jud 7-8; Luke 5:1-16
- ☐ Day 89: Jud 9-10; Luke 5:17-39
- ☐ Day 90: Jud 11-12; Luke 6:1-26
- ☐ Day 91: Jud 13-15; Luke 6:27-49
- ☐ Day 92: Jud 16-18; Luke 7:1-30
- ☐ Day 93: Jud 19-21; Luke 7:31-50
- ☐ Day 94: Ruth 1-4; Luke 8:1-25
- ☐ Day 95: 1Sam 1-3; Luke 8:26-56
- ☐ Day 96: 1Sam 4-6; Luke 9:1-17
- ☐ Day 97: 1Sam 7-9; Luke 9:18-36
- ☐ Day 98: 1Sam 10-12; Luke 9:37-62
- ☐ Day 99: 1Sam 13-14; Luke 10:1-24
- ☐ Day 100: 1Sam 15-16; Luke 10:25-42
- ☐ Day 101: 1Sam 17-18; Luke 11:1-28
- ☐ Day 102: 1Sam 19-21; Luke 11:29-54
- ☐ Day 103: 1Sam 22-24; Luke 12:1-31
- ☐ Day 104: 1Sam 25-26; Luke 12:32-59
- ☐ Day 105: 1Sam 27-29; Luke 13:1-22
- ☐ Day 106: 1Sam 30-31; Luke 13:23-35
- ☐ Day 107: 2Sam 1-2; Luke 14:1-24
- ☐ Day 108: 2Sam 3-5; Luke 14:25-35
- ☐ Day 109: 2Sam 6-8; Luke 15:1-10
- ☐ Day 110: 2Sam 9-11; Luke 15:11-32
- ☐ Day 111: 2Sam 12-13; Luke 16
- ☐ Day 112: 2Sam 14-15; Luke 17:1-19
- ☐ Day 113: 2Sam 16-18; Luke 17:20-37
- ☐ Day 114: 2Sam 19-20; Luke 18:1-23
- ☐ Day 115: 2Sam 21-22; Luke 18:24-43
- ☐ Day 116: 2Sam 23-24; Luke 19:1-27
- ☐ Day 117: 1King 1-2; Luke 19:28-48
- ☐ Day 118: 1King 3-5; Luke 20:1-26
- ☐ Day 119: 1King 6-7; Luke 20:27-47
- ☐ Day 120: 1King 8-9; Luke 21:1-19
- ☐ Day 121: 1King 10-11; Luke 21:20-38
- ☐ Day 122: 1King 12-13; Luke 22:1-30
- ☐ Day 123: 1King 14-15; Luke 22:31-46
- ☐ Day 124: 1King 16-18; Luke 22:47-71
- ☐ Day 125: 1King 19-20; Luke 23:1-25
- ☐ Day 126: 1King 21-22; Luke 23:26-56
- ☐ Day 127: 2King 1-3; Luke 24:1-35
- ☐ Day 128: 2King 4-6; Luke 24:36-53
- ☐ Day 129: 2King 7-9; John 1:1-28
- ☐ Day 130: 2King 10-12; John 1:29-51
- ☐ Day 131: 2King 13-14; John 2
- ☐ Day 132: 2King 15-16; John 3:1-18
- ☐ Day 133: 2King 17-18; John 3:19-36
- ☐ Day 134: 2King 19-21; John 4:1-30
- ☐ Day 135: 2King 22-23; John 4:31-54
- ☐ Day 136: 2King 24-25; John 5:1-24
- ☐ Day 137: 1Chron 1-3; John 5:25-47
- ☐ Day 138: 1Chron 4-6; John 6:1-21
- ☐ Day 139: 1Chron 7-9; John 6:22-44
- ☐ Day 140: 1Chron 10-12; John 6:45-71
- ☐ Day 141: 1Chron 13-15; John 7:1-27
- ☐ Day 142: 1Chron 16-18; John 7:28-53

- ☐ Day 143: 1Chron 19-21; John 8:1-27
- ☐ Day 144: 1Chron 22-24; John 8:28-59
- ☐ Day 145: 1Chron 25-27; John 9:1-23
- ☐ Day 146: 1Chron 28-29; John 9:24-41
- ☐ Day 147: 2Chron 1-3; John 10:1-23
- ☐ Day 148: 2Chron 4-6; John 10:24-42
- ☐ Day 149: 2Chron 7-9; John 11:1-29
- ☐ Day 150: 2Chron 10-12; John 11:30-57
- ☐ Day 151: 2Chron 13-14; John 12:1-26
- ☐ Day 153: 2Chron 15-16; John 12:27-50
- ☐ Day 153: 2Chron 17-18; John 13:1-20
- ☐ Day 154: 2Chron 19-20; John 13:21-38
- ☐ Day 155: 2Chron 21-22; John 14
- ☐ Day 156: 2Chron 23-24; John 15
- ☐ Day 157: 2Chron 25-27; John 16
- ☐ Day 158: 2Chron 28-29; John 17
- ☐ Day 159: 2Chron 30-31; John 18:1-18
- ☐ Day 160: 2Chron 32-33; John 18:19-40
- ☐ Day 161: 2Chron 34-36; John 19:1-22
- ☐ Day 162: Ezra 1-2; John 19:23-42
- ☐ Day 163: Ezra 3-5; John 20
- ☐ Day 164: Ezra 6-8; John 21
- ☐ Day 165: Ezra 9-10; Acts 1
- ☐ Day 166: Nehemiah 1-3; Acts 2:1-21
- ☐ Day 167: Nehemiah 4-6; Acts 2:22-47
- ☐ Day 168: Nehemiah 7-9; Acts 3
- ☐ Day 169: Nehemiah 10-11; Acts 4:1-22
- ☐ Day 170: Nehemiah 12-13; Acts 4:23-37
- ☐ Day 171: Esther 1-2; Acts 5:1-21
- ☐ Day 172: Esther 3-5; Acts 5:22-42
- ☐ Day 173: Esther 6-8; Acts 6
- ☐ Day 174: Esther 9-10; Acts 7:1-21
- ☐ Day 175: Job 1-2; Acts 7:22-43
- ☐ Day 176: Job 3-4; Acts 7:44-60
- ☐ Day 177: Job 5-7; Acts 8:1-25
- ☐ Day 178: Job 8-10; Acts 8:26-40
- ☐ Day 179: Job 11-13; Acts 9:1-21
- ☐ Day 180: Job 14-16; Acts 9:22-43
- ☐ Day 181: Job 17-19; Acts 10:1-23
- ☐ Day 182: Job 20-21; Acts 10:24-48

- ☐ Day 183: Job 22-24; Acts 11
- ☐ Day 184: Job 25-27; Acts 12
- ☐ Day 185: Job 28-29; Acts 13:1-25
- ☐ Day 186: Job 30-31; Acts 13:26-52
- ☐ Day 187: Job 32-33; Acts 14
- ☐ Day 188: Job 34-35; Acts 15:1-21
- ☐ Day 189: Job 36-37; Acts 15:22-41
- ☐ Day 190: Job 38-40; Acts 16:1-21
- ☐ Day 191: Job 41-42; Acts 16:22-40
- ☐ Day 192: Ps 1-3; Acts 17:1-15
- ☐ Day 193: Ps 4-6; Acts 17:16-34
- ☐ Day 194: Ps 7-9; Acts 18
- ☐ Day 195: Ps 10-12; Acts 19:1-20
- ☐ Day 196: Ps 13-15; Acts 19:21-41
- ☐ Day 197: Ps 16-17; Acts 20:1-16
- ☐ Day 198: Ps 18-19; Acts 20:17-38
- ☐ Day 199: Ps 20-22; Acts 21:1-17
- ☐ Day 200: Ps 23-25; Acts 21:18-40
- ☐ Day 201: Ps 26-28; Acts 22
- ☐ Day 202: Ps 29-30; Acts 23:1-15
- ☐ Day 203: Ps 31-32; Acts 23:16-35
- ☐ Day 204: Ps 33-34; Acts 24
- ☐ Day 205: Ps 35-36; Acts 25
- ☐ Day 206: Ps 37-39; Acts 26
- ☐ Day 207: Ps 40-42; Acts 27:1-26
- ☐ Day 208: Ps 43-45; Acts 27:27-44
- ☐ Day 209: Ps 46-48; Acts 28
- ☐ Day 210: Ps 49-50; Rom 1
- ☐ Day 211: Ps 51-53; Rom 2
- ☐ Day 212: Ps 54-56; Rom 3
- ☐ Day 213: Aug 1: Ps 57-59; Rom 4
- ☐ Day 214: Ps 60-62; Rom 5
- ☐ Day 215: Ps 63-65; Rom 6
- ☐ Day 216: Ps 66-67; Rom 7
- ☐ Day 217: Ps 68-69; Rom 8:1-21
- ☐ Day 218: Ps 70-71; Rom 8:22-39
- ☐ Day 219: Ps 72-73; Rom 9:1-15
- ☐ Day 220: Ps 74-76; Rom 9:16-33
- ☐ Day 221: Ps 77-78; Rom 10
- ☐ Day 222: Ps 79-80; Rom 11:1-18

☐ Day 223: Ps 81-83; Rom 11:19-36
☐ Day 224: Ps 84-86; Rom 12
☐ Day 225: Ps 87-88; Rom 13
☐ Day 226: Ps 89-90; Rom 14
☐ Day 227: Ps 91-93; Rom 15:1-13
☐ Day 228: Ps 94-96; Rom 15:14-33
☐ Day 229: Ps 97-99; Rom 16
☐ Day 230: Ps 100-102; 1Cor 1
☐ Day 231: Ps 103-104; 1Cor 2
☐ Day 232: Ps 105-106; 1Cor 3
☐ Day 233: Ps 107-109; 1Cor 4
☐ Day 234: Ps 110-112; 1Cor 5
☐ Day 235: Ps 113-115; 1Cor 6
☐ Day 236: Ps 116-118; 1Cor 7:1-19
☐ Day 237: Ps 119:1-88; 1Cor 7:20-40
☐ Day 238: Ps 119:89-176; 1Cor 8
☐ Day 239: Ps 120-122; 1Cor 9
☐ Day 240: Ps 123-125; 1Cor 10:1-18
☐ Day 241: Ps 126-128; 1Cor 10:19-33
☐ Day 242: Ps 129-131; 1Cor 11:1-16
☐ Day 243: Ps 132-134; 1Cor 11:17-34
☐ Day 244: Ps 135-136; 1Cor 12
☐ Day 245: Ps 137-139; 1Cor 13
☐ Day 246: Ps 140-142; 1Cor 14:1-20
☐ Day 247: Ps 143-145; 1Cor 14:21-40
☐ Day 248: Ps 146-147; 1Cor 15:1-28
☐ Day 249: Ps 148-150; 1Cor 15:29-58
☐ Day 250: Prov 1-2; 1Cor 16
☐ Day 251: Prov 3-5; 2Cor 1
☐ Day 252: Prov 6-7; 2Cor 2
☐ Day 253: Prov 8-9; 2Cor 3
☐ Day 254: Prov 10-12; 2Cor 4
☐ Day 255: Prov 13-15; 2Cor 5
☐ Day 256: Prov 16-18; 2Cor 6
☐ Day 257: Prov 19-21; 2Cor 7
☐ Day 258: Prov 22-24; 2Cor 8
☐ Day 259: Prov 25-26; 2Cor 9
☐ Day 260: Prov 27-29; 2Cor 10
☐ Day 261: Prov 30-31; 2Cor 11:1-15
☐ Day 262: Ecc 1-3; 2Cor 11:16-33

☐ Day 263: Ecc 4-6; 2Cor 12
☐ Day 264: Ecc 7-9; 2Cor 13
☐ Day 265: Ecc 10-12; Gal 1
☐ Day 266: Song 1-3; Gal 2
☐ Day 267: Song 4-5; Gal 3
☐ Day 268: Song 6-8; Gal 4
☐ Day 269: Is 1-2; Gal 5
☐ Day 270: Is 3-4; Gal 6
☐ Day 271: Is 5-6; Eph 1
☐ Day 272: Is 7-8; Eph 2
☐ Day 273: Is 9-10; Eph 3
☐ Day 274: Is 11-13; Eph 4
☐ Day 275: Is 14-16; Eph 5:1-16
☐ Day 276: Is 17-19; Eph 5:17-33
☐ Day 277: Is 20-22; Eph 6
☐ Day 278: Is 23-25; Phil 1
☐ Day 279: Is 26-27; Phil 2
☐ Day 280: Is 28-29; Phil 3
☐ Day 281 : Is 30-31; Phil 4
☐ Day 282: Is 32-33; Col 1
☐ Day 283: Is 34-36; Col 2
☐ Day 284: Is 37-38; Col 3
☐ Day 285: Is 39-40; Col 4
☐ Day 286: Is 41-42; 1Thess 1
☐ Day 287: Is 43-44; 1Thess 2
☐ Day 288: Is 45-46; 1Thess 3
☐ Day 289: Is 47-49; 1Thess 4
☐ Day 290: Is 50-52; 1Thess 5
☐ Day 291: Is 53-55; 2Thess 1
☐ Day 292: Is 56-58; 2Thess 2
☐ Day 293: Is 59-61; 2Thess 3
☐ Day 294: Is 62-64; 1Tim 1
☐ Day 295: Is 65-66; 1Tim 2
☐ Day 296: Jer 1-2; 1Tim 3
☐ Day 297: Jer 3-5; 1Tim 4
☐ Day 298: Jer 6-8; 1Tim 5
☐ Day 299: Jer 9-11; 1Tim 6
☐ Day 300: Jer 12-14; 2Tim 1
☐ Day 301: Jer 15-17; 2Tim 2
☐ Day 302: Jer 18-19; 2Tim 3

- ☐ Day 303: Jer 20-21; 2Tim 4
- ☐ Day 304: Jer 22-23; Titus 1
- ☐ Day 305: Jer 24-26; Titus 2
- ☐ Day 306: Jer 27-29; Titus 3
- ☐ Day 307: Jer 30-31; Philemon
- ☐ Day 308: Jer 32-33; Heb 1
- ☐ Day 309: Jer 34-36; Heb 2
- ☐ Day 310: Jer 37-39; Heb 3
- ☐ Day 311: Jer 40-42; Heb 4
- ☐ Day 312: Jer 43-45; Heb 5
- ☐ Day 313: Jer 46-47; Heb 6
- ☐ Day 314: Jer 48-49; Heb 7
- ☐ Day 315: Jer 50; Heb 8
- ☐ Day 316: Jer 51-52; Heb 9
- ☐ Day 317: Lam 1-2; Heb 10:1-18
- ☐ Day 318: Lam 3-5; Heb 10:19-39
- ☐ Day 319: Ezek 1-2; Heb 11:1-19
- ☐ Day 320: Ezek 3-4; Heb 11:20-40
- ☐ Day 321: Ezek 5-7; Heb 12
- ☐ Day 322: Ezek 8-10; Heb 13
- ☐ Day 323: Ezek 11-13; James 1
- ☐ Day 324: Ezek 14-15; James 2
- ☐ Day 325: Ezek 16-17; James 3
- ☐ Day 326: Ezek 18-19; James 4
- ☐ Day 327: Ezek 20-21; James 5
- ☐ Day 328: Ezek 22-23; 1Pet 1
- ☐ Day 329: Ezek 24-26; 1Pet 2
- ☐ Day 330: Ezek 27-29; 1Pet 3
- ☐ Day 331: Ezek 30-32; 1Pet 4
- ☐ Day 332: Ezek 33-34; 1Pet 5
- ☐ Day 333: Ezek 35-36; 2Pet 1
- ☐ Day 334: Ezek 37-39; 2Pet 2
- ☐ Day 335: Ezek 40-41; 2Pet 3
- ☐ Day 336: Ezek 42-44; 1John 1
- ☐ Day 337: Ezek 45-46; 1John 2
- ☐ Day 338: Ezek 47-48; 1John 3
- ☐ Day 339: Dan 1-2; 1John 4
- ☐ Day 340: Dan 3-4; 1John 5
- ☐ Day 341: Dan 5-7; 2John
- ☐ Day 342: Dan 8-10; 3John

- ☐ Day 343: Dan 11-12; Jude
- ☐ Day 344: Hosea 1-4; Rev 1
- ☐ Day 345: Hosea 5-8; Rev 2
- ☐ Day 346: Hosea 9-11; Rev 3
- ☐ Day 347: Hosea 12-14; Rev 4
- ☐ Day 348: Joel; Rev 5
- ☐ Day 349: Amos 1-3; Rev 6
- ☐ Day 350: Amos 4-6; Rev 7
- ☐ Day 351: Amos 7-9; Rev 8
- ☐ Day 352: Obadiah; Rev 9
- ☐ Day 353: Jonah; Rev 10
- ☐ Day 354: Micah 1-3; Rev 11
- ☐ Day 355: Micah 4-5; Rev 12
- ☐ Day 356: Micah 6-7; Rev 13
- ☐ Day 357: Nahum; Rev 14
- ☐ Day 358: Habakkuk; Rev 15
- ☐ Day 359: Zephaniah; Rev 16
- ☐ Day 360: Haggai; Rev 17
- ☐ Day 361: Zech 1-4; Rev 18
- ☐ Day 362: Zech 5-8; Rev 19
- ☐ Day 363: Zech 9-12; Rev 20
- ☐ Day 364: Zech 13-14; Rev 21
- ☐ Day 365: Malachi; Rev 22

Calendar Reading Plan

This reading plan is for the person who wants to read through the Holy Scriptures in an entire calendar year. Though the pace is steady, you will find it is still doable and reasonable. And in one year, you will have read through the entire Bible, perhaps for the first time!

- ☐ Jan 1: Gen 1-3; Matt 1
- ☐ Jan 2: Gen 4-6; Matt 2
- ☐ Jan 3: Gen 7-9; Matt 3
- ☐ Jan 4: Gen 10-12; Matt 4
- ☐ Jan 5: Gen 13-15; Matt 5:1-26
- ☐ Jan 6: Gen 16-17; Matt 5:27-48
- ☐ Jan 7: Gen 18-19; Matt 6:1-18
- ☐ Jan 8: Gen 20-22; Matt 6:19-34
- ☐ Jan 9: Gen 23-24; Matt 7
- ☐ Jan 10: Gen 25-26; Matt 8:1-17
- ☐ Jan 11: Gen 27-28; Matt 8:18-34
- ☐ Jan 12: Gen 29-30; Matt 9:1-17
- ☐ Jan 13: Gen 31-32; Matt 9:18-38
- ☐ Jan 14: Gen 33-35; Matt 10:1-20
- ☐ Jan 15: Gen 36-38; Matt 10:21-42
- ☐ Jan 16: Gen 39-40; Matt 11
- ☐ Jan 17: Gen 41-42; Matt 12:1-23
- ☐ Jan 18: Gen 43-45; Matt 12:24-50
- ☐ Jan 19: Gen 46-48; Matt 13:1-30
- ☐ Jan 20: Gen 49-50; Matt 13:31-58
- ☐ Jan 21: Ex 1-3; Matt 14:1-21
- ☐ Jan 22: Ex 4-6; Matt 14:22-36
- ☐ Jan 23: Ex 7-8; Matt 15:1-20
- ☐ Jan 24: Ex 9-11; Matt 15:21-39
- ☐ Jan 25: Ex 12-13; Matt 16
- ☐ Jan 26: Ex 14-15; Matt 17
- ☐ Jan 27: Ex 16-18; Matt 18:1-20
- ☐ Jan 28: Ex 19-20; Matt 18:21-35
- ☐ Jan 29: Ex 21-22; Matt 19
- ☐ Jan 30: Ex 23-24; Matt 20:1-16
- ☐ Jan 31: Ex 25-26; Matt 20:17-34

- ☐ Feb 1: Ex 27-28; Matt 21:1-22
- ☐ Feb 2: Ex 29-30; Matt 21:23-46
- ☐ Feb 3: Ex 31-33; Matt 22: 1-22
- ☐ Feb 4: Ex 34-35; Matt 22:23-46
- ☐ Feb 5: Ex 36-38; Matt 23:1-22
- ☐ Feb 6: Ex 39-40; Matt 23:23-39
- ☐ Feb 7: Lev 1-3; Matt 24:1-28
- ☐ Feb 8: Lev 4-5; Matt 24:29-51
- ☐ Feb 9: Lev 6-7; Matt 25:1-30
- ☐ Feb 10: Lev 8-10; Matt 25:31-46
- ☐ Feb 11: Lev 11-12; Matt 26:1-25
- ☐ Feb 12: Lev 13; Matt 26:26-50
- ☐ Feb 13: Lev 14; Matt 26:51-75
- ☐ Feb 14: Lev 15-16; Matt 27:1-26
- ☐ Feb 15: Lev 17-18; Matt 27:27-50
- ☐ Feb 16: Lev 19-20; Matt 27:51-66
- ☐ Feb 17: Lev 21-22; Matt 28
- ☐ Feb 18: Lev 23-24; Mark 1:1-22
- ☐ Feb 19: Lev 25; Mark 1:23-45
- ☐ Feb 20: Lev 26-27; Mark 2
- ☐ Feb 21: Num 1-2; Mark 3:1-19
- ☐ Feb 22: Num 3-4; Mark 3:20-35
- ☐ Feb 23: Num 5-6; Mark 4:1-20
- ☐ Feb 24: Num 7-8; Mark 4:21-41
- ☐ Feb 25: Num 9-11; Mark 5:1-20
- ☐ Feb 26: Num 12-14; Mark 5:21-43
- ☐ Feb 27: Num 15-16; Mark 6:1-29
- ☐ Feb 28/29: Num 17-19; Mark 6:30-56
- ☐ Mar 1: Num 20-22; Mark 7:1-13
- ☐ Mar 2: Num 23-25; Mark 7:14-37
- ☐ Mar 3: Num 26-28; Mark 8

- [ ] Mar 4: Num 29-31; Mark 9:1-29
- [ ] Mar 5: Num 32-34; Mark 9:30-50
- [ ] Mar 6: Num 35-36; Mark 10:1-31
- [ ] Mar 7: Deut 1-3; Mark 10:32-52
- [ ] Mar 8: Deut 4-6; Mark 11:1-18
- [ ] Mar 9: Deut 7-9; Mark 11:19-33
- [ ] Mar 10: Deut 10-12; Mark 12:1-27
- [ ] Mar 11: Deut 13-15; Mark 12:28-44
- [ ] Mar 12: Deut 16-18; Mark 13:1-20
- [ ] Mar 13: Deut 19-21; Mark 13:21-37
- [ ] Mar 14: Deut 22-24; Mark 14:1-26
- [ ] Mar 15: Deut 25-27; Mark 14:27-53
- [ ] Mar 16: Deut 28-29; Mark 14:54-72
- [ ] Mar 17: Deut 30-31; Mark 15:1-25
- [ ] Mar 18: Deut 32-34; Mark 15:26-47
- [ ] Mar 19: Josh 1-3; Mark 16
- [ ] Mar 20: Josh 4-6; Luke 1:1-20
- [ ] Mar 21: Josh 7-9; Luke 1:21-38
- [ ] Mar 22: Josh 10-12; Luke 1:39-56
- [ ] Mar 23: Josh 13-15; Luke 1:57-80
- [ ] Mar 24: Josh 16-18; Luke 2:1-24
- [ ] Mar 25: Josh 19-21; Luke 2:25-52
- [ ] Mar 26: Josh 22-24; Luke 3
- [ ] Mar 27: Jud 1-3; Luke 4:1-30
- [ ] Mar 28: Jud 4-6; Luke 4:31-44
- [ ] Mar 29: Jud 7-8; Luke 5:1-16
- [ ] Mar 30: Jud 9-10; Luke 5:17-39
- [ ] Mar 31: Jud 11-12; Luke 6:1-26
- [ ] Apr 1: Jud 13-15; Luke 6:27-49
- [ ] Apr 2: Jud 16-18; Luke 7:1-30
- [ ] Apr 3: Jud 19-21; Luke 7:31-50
- [ ] Apr 4: Ruth 1-4; Luke 8:1-25
- [ ] Apr 5: 1Sam 1-3; Luke 8:26-56
- [ ] Apr 6: 1Sam 4-6; Luke 9:1-17
- [ ] Apr 7: 1Sam 7-9; Luke 9:18-36
- [ ] Apr 8: 1Sam 10-12; Luke 9:37-62
- [ ] Apr 9: 1Sam 13-14; Luke 10:1-24
- [ ] Apr 10: 1Sam 15-16; Luke 10:25-42
- [ ] Apr 11: 1Sam 17-18; Luke 11:1-28
- [ ] Apr 12: 1Sam 19-21; Luke 11:29-54
- [ ] Apr 13: 1Sam 22-24; Luke 12:1-31
- [ ] Apr 14: 1Sam 25-26; Luke 12:32-59
- [ ] Apr 15: 1Sam 27-29; Luke 13:1-22
- [ ] Apr 16: 1Sam 30-31; Luke 13:23-35
- [ ] Apr 17: 2Sam 1-2; Luke 14:1-24
- [ ] Apr 18: 2Sam 3-5; Luke 14:25-35
- [ ] Apr 19: 2Sam 6-8; Luke 15:1-10
- [ ] Apr 20: 2Sam 9-11; Luke 15:11-32
- [ ] Apr 21: 2Sam 12-13; Luke 16
- [ ] Apr 22: 2Sam 14-15; Luke 17:1-19
- [ ] Apr 23: 2Sam 16-18; Luke 17:20-37
- [ ] Apr 24: 2Sam 19-20; Luke 18:1-23
- [ ] Apr 25: 2Sam 21-22; Luke 18:24-43
- [ ] Apr 26: 2Sam 23-24; Luke 19:1-27
- [ ] Apr 27: 1King 1-2; Luke 19:28-48
- [ ] Apr 28: 1King 3-5; Luke 20:1-26
- [ ] Apr 29: 1King 6-7; Luke 20:27-47
- [ ] Apr 30: 1King 8-9; Luke 21:1-19
- [ ] May 1: 1King 10-11; Luke 21:20-38
- [ ] May 2: 1King 12-13; Luke 22:1-30
- [ ] May 3: 1King 14-15; Luke 22:31-46
- [ ] May 4: 1King 16-18; Luke 22:47-71
- [ ] May 5: 1King 19-20; Luke 23:1-25
- [ ] May 6: 1King 21-22; Luke 23:26-56
- [ ] May 7: 2King 1-3; Luke 24:1-35
- [ ] May 8: 2King 4-6; Luke 24:36-53
- [ ] May 9: 2King 7-9; John 1:1-28
- [ ] May 10: 2King 10-12; John 1:29-51
- [ ] May 11: 2King 13-14; John 2
- [ ] May 12: 2King 15-16; John 3:1-18
- [ ] May 13: 2King 17-18; John 3:19-36
- [ ] May 14: 2King 19-21; John 4:1-30
- [ ] May 15: 2King 22-23; John 4:31-54
- [ ] May 16: 2King 24-25; John 5:1-24
- [ ] May 17: 1Chron 1-3; John 5:25-47
- [ ] May 18: 1Chron 4-6; John 6:1-21
- [ ] May 19: 1Chron 7-9; John 6:22-44
- [ ] May 20: 1Chron 10-12; John 6:45-71
- [ ] May 21: 1Chron 13-15; John 7:1-27
- [ ] May 22: 1Chron 16-18; John 7:28-53

- [ ] May 23: 1Chron 19-21; John 8:1-27
- [ ] May 24: 1Chron 22-24; John 8:28-59
- [ ] May 25: 1Chron 25-27; John 9:1-23
- [ ] May 26: 1Chron 28-29; John 9:24-41
- [ ] May 27: 2Chron 1-3; John 10:1-23
- [ ] May 28: 2Chron 4-6; John 10:24-42
- [ ] May 29: 2Chron 7-9; John 11:1-29
- [ ] May 30: 2Chron 10-12; John 11:30-57
- [ ] May 31: 2Chron 13-14; John 12:1-26
- [ ] Jun 1: 2Chron 15-16; John 12:27-50
- [ ] Jun 2: 2Chron 17-18; John 13:1-20
- [ ] Jun 3: 2Chron 19-20; John 13:21-38
- [ ] Jun 4: 2Chron 21-22; John 14
- [ ] Jun 5: 2Chron 23-24; John 15
- [ ] Jun 6: 2Chron 25-27; John 16
- [ ] Jun 7: 2Chron 28-29; John 17
- [ ] Jun 8: 2Chron 30-31; John 18:1-18
- [ ] Jun 9: 2Chron 32-33; John 18:19-40
- [ ] Jun 10: 2Chron 34-36; John 19:1-22
- [ ] Jun 11: Ezra 1-2; John 19:23-42
- [ ] Jun 12: Ezra 3-5; John 20
- [ ] Jun 13: Ezra 6-8; John 21
- [ ] Jun 14: Ezra 9-10; Acts 1
- [ ] Jun 15: Nehemiah 1-3; Acts 2:1-21
- [ ] Jun 16: Nehemiah 4-6; Acts 2:22-47
- [ ] Jun 17: Nehemiah 7-9; Acts 3
- [ ] Jun 18: Nehemiah 10-11; Acts 4:1-22
- [ ] Jun 19: Nehemiah 12-13; Acts 4:23-37
- [ ] Jun 20: Esther 1-2; Acts 5:1-21
- [ ] Jun 21: Esther 3-5; Acts 5:22-42
- [ ] Jun 22: Esther 6-8; Acts 6
- [ ] Jun 23: Esther 9-10; Acts 7:1-21
- [ ] Jun 24: Job 1-2; Acts 7:22-43
- [ ] Jun 25: Job 3-4; Acts 7:44-60
- [ ] Jun 26: Job 5-7; Acts 8:1-25
- [ ] Jun 27: Job 8-10; Acts 8:26-40
- [ ] Jun 28: Job 11-13; Acts 9:1-21
- [ ] Jun 29: Job 14-16; Acts 9:22-43
- [ ] Jun 30: Job 17-19; Acts 10:1-23
- [ ] Jul 1: Job 20-21; Acts 10:24-48
- [ ] Jul 2: Job 22-24; Acts 11
- [ ] Jul 3: Job 25-27; Acts 12
- [ ] Jul 4: Job 28-29; Acts 13:1-25
- [ ] Jul 5: Job 30-31; Acts 13:26-52
- [ ] Jul 6: Job 32-33; Acts 14
- [ ] Jul 7: Job 34-35; Acts 15:1-21
- [ ] Jul 8: Job 36-37; Acts 15:22-41
- [ ] Jul 9: Job 38-40; Acts 16:1-21
- [ ] Jul 10: Job 41-42; Acts 16:22-40
- [ ] Jul 11: Ps 1-3; Acts 17:1-15
- [ ] Jul 12: Ps 4-6; Acts 17:16-34
- [ ] Jul 13: Ps 7-9; Acts 18
- [ ] Jul 14: Ps 10-12; Acts 19:1-20
- [ ] Jul 15: Ps 13-15; Acts 19:21-41
- [ ] Jul 16: Ps 16-17; Acts 20:1-16
- [ ] Jul 17: Ps 18-19; Acts 20:17-38
- [ ] Jul 18: Ps 20-22; Acts 21:1-17
- [ ] Jul 19: Ps 23-25; Acts 21:18-40
- [ ] Jul 20: Ps 26-28; Acts 22
- [ ] Jul 21: Ps 29-30; Acts 23:1-15
- [ ] Jul 22: Ps 31-32; Acts 23:16-35
- [ ] Jul 23: Ps 33-34; Acts 24
- [ ] Jul 24: Ps 35-36; Acts 25
- [ ] Jul 25: Ps 37-39; Acts 26
- [ ] Jul 26: Ps 40-42; Acts 27:1-26
- [ ] Jul 27: Ps 43-45; Acts 27:27-44
- [ ] Jul 28: Ps 46-48; Acts 28
- [ ] Jul 29: Ps 49-50; Rom 1
- [ ] Jul 30: Ps 51-53; Rom 2
- [ ] Jul 31: Ps 54-56; Rom 3
- [ ] Aug 1: Ps 57-59; Rom 4
- [ ] Aug 2: Ps 60-62; Rom 5
- [ ] Aug 3: Ps 63-65; Rom 6
- [ ] Aug 4: Ps 66-67; Rom 7
- [ ] Aug 5: Ps 68-69; Rom 8:1-21
- [ ] Aug 6: Ps 70-71; Rom 8:22-39
- [ ] Aug 7: Ps 72-73; Rom 9:1-15
- [ ] Aug 8: Ps 74-76; Rom 9:16-33
- [ ] Aug 9: Ps 77-78; Rom 10
- [ ] Aug 10: Ps 79-80; Rom 11:1-18

PRAYERS FOR MY CITY

- [ ] Aug 11: Ps 81-83; Rom 11:19-36
- [ ] Aug 12: Ps 84-86; Rom 12
- [ ] Aug 13: Ps 87-88; Rom 13
- [ ] Aug 14: Ps 89-90; Rom 14
- [ ] Aug 15: Ps 91-93; Rom 15:1-13
- [ ] Aug 16: Ps 94-96; Rom 15:14-33
- [ ] Aug 17: Ps 97-99; Rom 16
- [ ] Aug 18: Ps 100-102; 1Cor 1
- [ ] Aug 19: Ps 103-104; 1Cor 2
- [ ] Aug 20: Ps 105-106; 1Cor 3
- [ ] Aug 21: Ps 107-109; 1Cor 4
- [ ] Aug 22: Ps 110-112; 1Cor 5
- [ ] Aug 23: Ps 113-115; 1Cor 6
- [ ] Aug 24: Ps 116-118; 1Cor 7:1-19
- [ ] Aug 25: Ps 119:1-88; 1Cor 7:20-40
- [ ] Aug 26: Ps 119:89-176; 1Cor 8
- [ ] Aug 27: Ps 120-122; 1Cor 9
- [ ] Aug 28: Ps 123-125; 1Cor 10:1-18
- [ ] Aug 29: Ps 126-128; 1Cor 10:19-33
- [ ] Aug 30: Ps 129-131; 1Cor 11:1-16
- [ ] Aug 31: Ps 132-134; 1Cor 11:17-34
- [ ] Sep 1: Ps 135-136; 1Cor 12
- [ ] Sep 2: Ps 137-139; 1Cor 13
- [ ] Sep 3: Ps 140-142; 1Cor 14:1-20
- [ ] Sep 4: Ps 143-145; 1Cor 14:21-40
- [ ] Sep 5: Ps 146-147; 1Cor 15:1-28
- [ ] Sep 6: Ps 148-150; 1Cor 15:29-58
- [ ] Sep 7: Prov 1-2; 1Cor 16
- [ ] Sep 8: Prov 3-5; 2Cor 1
- [ ] Sep 9: Prov 6-7; 2Cor 2
- [ ] Sep 10: Prov 8-9; 2Cor 3
- [ ] Sep 11: Prov 10-12; 2Cor 4
- [ ] Sep 12: Prov 13-15; 2Cor 5
- [ ] Sep 13: Prov 16-18; 2Cor 6
- [ ] Sep 14: Prov 19-21; 2Cor 7
- [ ] Sep 15: Prov 22-24; 2Cor 8
- [ ] Sep 16: Prov 25-26; 2Cor 9
- [ ] Sep 17: Prov 27-29; 2Cor 10
- [ ] Sep 18: Prov 30-31; 2Cor 11:1-15
- [ ] Sep 19: Ecc 1-3; 2Cor 11:16-33

- [ ] Sep 20: Ecc 4-6; 2Cor 12
- [ ] Sep 21: Ecc 7-9; 2Cor 13
- [ ] Sep 22: Ecc 10-12; Gal 1
- [ ] Sep 23: Song 1-3; Gal 2
- [ ] Sep 24: Song 4-5; Gal 3
- [ ] Sep 25: Song 6-8; Gal 4
- [ ] Sep 26: Is 1-2; Gal 5
- [ ] Sep 27: Is 3-4; Gal 6
- [ ] Sep 28: Is 5-6; Eph 1
- [ ] Sep 29: Is 7-8; Eph 2
- [ ] Sep 30: Is 9-10; Eph 3
- [ ] Oct 1: Is 11-13; Eph 4
- [ ] Oct 2: Is 14-16; Eph 5:1-16
- [ ] Oct 3: Is 17-19; Eph 5:17-33
- [ ] Oct 4: Is 20-22; Eph 6
- [ ] Oct 5: Is 23-25; Phil 1
- [ ] Oct 6: Is 26-27; Phil 2
- [ ] Oct 7: Is 28-29; Phil 3
- [ ] Oct 8: Is 30-31; Phil 4
- [ ] Oct 9: Is 32-33; Col 1
- [ ] Oct 10: Is 34-36; Col 2
- [ ] Oct 11: Is 37-38; Col 3
- [ ] Oct 12: Is 39-40; Col 4
- [ ] Oct 13: Is 41-42; 1Thess 1
- [ ] Oct 14: Is 43-44; 1Thess 2
- [ ] Oct 15: Is 45-46; 1Thess 3
- [ ] Oct 16: Is 47-49; 1Thess 4
- [ ] Oct 17: Is 50-52; 1Thess 5
- [ ] Oct 18: Is 53-55; 2Thess 1
- [ ] Oct 19: Is 56-58; 2Thess 2
- [ ] Oct 20: Is 59-61; 2Thess 3
- [ ] Oct 21: Is 62-64; 1Tim 1
- [ ] Oct 22: Is 65-66; 1Tim 2
- [ ] Oct 23: Jer 1-2; 1Tim 3
- [ ] Oct 24: Jer 3-5; 1Tim 4
- [ ] Oct 25: Jer 6-8; 1Tim 5
- [ ] Oct 26: Jer 9-11; 1Tim 6
- [ ] Oct 27: Jer 12-14; 2Tim 1
- [ ] Oct 28: Jer 15-17; 2Tim 2
- [ ] Oct 29: Jer 18-19; 2Tim 3

- ☐ Oct 30: Jer 20-21; 2Tim 4
- ☐ Oct 31: Jer 22-23; Titus 1
- ☐ Nov 1: Jer 24-26; Titus 2
- ☐ Nov 2: Jer 27-29; Titus 3
- ☐ Nov 3: Jer 30-31; Philemon
- ☐ Nov 4: Jer 32-33; Heb 1
- ☐ Nov 5: Jer 34-36; Heb 2
- ☐ Nov 6: Jer 37-39; Heb 3
- ☐ Nov 7: Jer 40-42; Heb 4
- ☐ Nov 8: Jer 43-45; Heb 5
- ☐ Nov 9: Jer 46-47; Heb 6
- ☐ Nov 10: Jer 48-49; Heb 7
- ☐ Nov 11: Jer 50; Heb 8
- ☐ Nov 12: Jer 51-52; Heb 9
- ☐ Nov 13: Lam 1-2; Heb 10:1-18
- ☐ Nov 14: Lam 3-5; Heb 10:19-39
- ☐ Nov 15: Ezek 1-2; Heb 11:1-19
- ☐ Nov 16: Ezek 3-4; Heb 11:20-40
- ☐ Nov 17: Ezek 5-7; Heb 12
- ☐ Nov 18: Ezek 8-10; Heb 13
- ☐ Nov 19: Ezek 11-13; James 1
- ☐ Nov 20: Ezek 14-15; James 2
- ☐ Nov 21: Ezek 16-17; James 3
- ☐ Nov 22: Ezek 18-19; James 4
- ☐ Nov 23: Ezek 20-21; James 5
- ☐ Nov 24: Ezek 22-23; 1Pet 1
- ☐ Nov 25: Ezek 24-26; 1Pet 2
- ☐ Nov 26: Ezek 27-29; 1Pet 3
- ☐ Nov 27: Ezek 30-32; 1Pet 4
- ☐ Nov 28: Ezek 33-34; 1Pet 5
- ☐ Nov 29: Ezek 35-36; 2Pet 1
- ☐ Nov 30: Ezek 37-39; 2Pet 2
- ☐ Dec 1: Ezek 40-41; 2Pet 3
- ☐ Dec 2: Ezek 42-44; 1John 1
- ☐ Dec 3: Ezek 45-46; 1John 2
- ☐ Dec 4: Ezek 47-48; 1John 3
- ☐ Dec 5: Dan 1-2; 1John 4
- ☐ Dec 6: Dan 3-4; 1John 5
- ☐ Dec 7: Dan 5-7; 2John
- ☐ Dec 8: Dan 8-10; 3John
- ☐ Dec 9: Dan 11-12; Jude
- ☐ Dec 10: Hosea 1-4; Rev 1
- ☐ Dec 11: Hosea 5-8; Rev 2
- ☐ Dec 12: Hosea 9-11; Rev 3
- ☐ Dec 13: Hosea 12-14; Rev 4
- ☐ Dec 14: Joel; Rev 5
- ☐ Dec 15: Amos 1-3; Rev 6
- ☐ Dec 16: Amos 4-6; Rev 7
- ☐ Dec 17: Amos 7-9; Rev 8
- ☐ Dec 18: Obadiah; Rev 9
- ☐ Dec 19: Jonah; Rev 10
- ☐ Dec 20: Micah 1-3; Rev 11
- ☐ Dec 21: Micah 4-5; Rev 12
- ☐ Dec 22: Micah 6-7; Rev 13
- ☐ Dec 23: Nahum; Rev 14
- ☐ Dec 24: Habakkuk; Rev 15
- ☐ Dec 25: Zephaniah; Rev 16
- ☐ Dec 26: Haggai; Rev 17
- ☐ Dec 27: Zech 1-4; Rev 18
- ☐ Dec 28: Zech 5-8; Rev 19
- ☐ Dec 29: Zech 9-12; Rev 20
- ☐ Dec 30: Zech 13-14; Rev 21
- ☐ Dec 31: Malachi; Rev 22

www.ingramcontent.com/pod-product-compliance
Lightning Source LLC
Chambersburg PA
CBHW071052040426
42443CB00013B/3315